WALK
THROUGH
HISTORY

WALK
THROUGH
HISTORY

VICTORIAN
LONDON

Christopher Winn

ILLUSTRATIONS BY
Mai Osawa

EBURY
PRESS

Ebury Press, an imprint of Ebury Publishing,
20 Vauxhall Bridge Road,
London SW1V 2SA

Ebury Press is part of the Penguin Random House group of companies
whose addresses can be found at global.penguinrandomhouse.com

Illustrations by Mai Osawa

First published by Ebury Press in 2018

www.penguin.co.uk

A CIP catalogue record for this book is available from the British Library

ISBN 9781785036897

Typeset in India by Integra Software Services Pvt. Ltd, Pondicherry

Printed and bound in Great Britain by Clays Ltd, St Ives PLC

Contents

Preface

For those who have eyes to see ...

*W*alk *through History: Victorian London* is an exciting new way to explore London afresh. Walking becomes an adventure, the streets become places of discovery and surprise, history comes alive.

Victorian London is all around us. And yet much of it goes unappreciated, hidden from view by familiarity and everyday life.

The London we live in today is, to all intents and purposes, Victorian London. Londoners live in Victorian houses, are taught in Victorian schools, worship in Victorian churches, are treated in Victorian hospitals, drink in Victorian pubs, play in Victorian parks and gardens, are entertained in Victorian theatres and Victorian museums, drive down Victorian streets, cross Victorian bridges and travel on Victorian railways.

Over the course of Queen Victoria's reign, between 1837 and 1901, London's population grew from something over one million to more than seven million people and the Victorians had to build a city that could accommodate such numbers. They cleared away the slums and laid out London's streets and public parks. They built the first social housing and the first effective sewerage system. They built the first proper schools and hospitals, the first libraries and museums, galleries and theatres, the first railway stations and public transport system. Inspired by Catholic Emancipation and the Anglican revival they built hundreds of churches and chapels. They built the first luxury apartment blocks and hotels. They built terraces and villas and cottages and studios. They built the great edifices of the modern state, the Houses of Parliament, the Government Offices, the Law Courts. They built the great monuments to commerce, the offices and warehouses, department stores and shopping streets and market places. They built the great monuments to finance, the banking halls and insurance halls and counting houses that made Victorian London into the world's leading financial centre, which it still is today. Immigration and trade from all over the world made Victorian London into the first world city, and it remains today the world's most cosmopolitan city.

Social and technological advances during the Victorian Age required new buildings for new purposes. Professional architects came into being to design them and different architects championed different styles.

At the beginning of the Victorian Age the predominant style was classical, based on ancient Greco-Roman architecture and reflected in the endless rows of stuccoed Italianate terraces of west London built in the 1840s and 50s.

As the Victorian Age progressed new technologies and building methods and materials gave architects a greater choice and the 'Battle of the Styles' developed, with Gothic Revival providing the greatest competition. The champions of the Gothic style, as developed by the medieval English church builders, regarded it as symbolic of Christianity, and thus Gothic became the style of choice for churches and for buildings associated with the Church, schools and hospitals and even those cathedrals of learning, museums. Gothic was also thought of as the purest form of English expression and hence was chosen as the design for the Houses of Parliament, perhaps the most distinctive national parliament building in the world. Architects such as Sir George Gilbert Scott and William Butterfield then elaborated on the Gothic and made it their own with polychrome bricks, terracotta and ironwork.

Conscious of the religious overtones of Gothic, the secular world largely stuck with classical, hence London's many Italianate and classical banking halls and head offices, clubs such as the Reform Club and the National Liberal Club, hotels such as the Charing Cross Hotel and the Grosvenor.

As London's population exploded, new kinds of domestic buildings were required. J.J. Stevenson and Norman Shaw developed mansion blocks and town houses in what became known as the Queen Anne style of red brick and stone. Sir Ernest George and Harold Peto favoured a flamboyant Flemish style with steep gables and tall chimneys. The Arts and Crafts movement developed its own style, harking back to the medieval world but free from the religious elements.

Each of these styles had within it many variations, and thus London is blessed with a greater variety of architecture than perhaps any other city on Earth. The vision and imagination and confidence that created Victorian London is breathtaking. The attention to detail on even the most mundane of buildings is extraordinary. The genius of Victorian engineering prowess is spectacular.

Although much of Victorian London has been lost to bombing and crass urban planning, organisations such as the Victorian Society and heroes such as Sir John Betjeman have ensured that much has also been saved – so much in fact that it would be impossible to cover it all. So, *Walk through History: Victorian London* cherry-picks the best of it for you, visiting some of the city's greatest Victorian treasures and leading you to some of the finest examples of Victorian London's many faces.

A note of warning. Walking through Victorian London can become addictive. Once your attention has been drawn to Victorian London you will see it everywhere. Never again will you be able to walk down a street blissfully unaware of that Victorian terrace or school or church. Never again will you be able to pass by a Victorian building without informing those around you of what architectural style it is and who the architect was and who lived and worked there. Never more will you be able to resist pointing out the detail, the varied window arches and ironwork, the terracotta and stone dressings, the polychrome brickwork, the statues and carvings and friezes.

And 'why,' you will ask yourself, 'have I never noticed that before?'

How to use
Walk through History: Victorian London

The walks in each of the seven chapters of this book cover different areas of central London, areas that serve different purposes, have a different atmosphere and possess different types of architecture. Although the walks in each chapter are contiguous and can be completed in one day, they have been designed to be walked in stages as well. How many walks to do and how long to take depends entirely upon the individual reader, how fast he or she walks, how much time is available, how much time the reader decides to spend at each attraction, how many breaks for refreshment are taken. Each walk never strays far from an underground station so that the reader may start and finish at any point on the walk. Recommended places for refreshment are marked on the map and, in most cases, featured in the text.

All I would advise is that the walks will inevitably take longer than you think – there is so much to see and, once attuned, readers may well find themselves wandering off to look at something that has caught their eye away from the main route.

Above all, I hope that *Walk through History: Victorian London,* will encourage you to want to walk but also to see.

The maps are not to scale and have been simplified for the sake of clarity, omitting unnecessary street names, but when in situ on the walk the map directions are easy to follow.

—

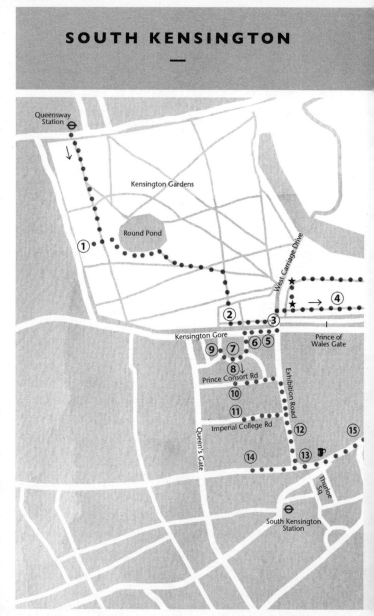

Queensway
Station

Kensington Gardens

Round Pond

West Carriage Drive

① ④

② ③

Kensington Gore
⑨ ⑦ ⑥ ⑤
⑧
Prince Consort Rd
⑩
⑪
Imperial College Rd

Prince of
Wales Gate

Exhibition Road

⑫ ⑮
⑬
⑭

Queen's Gate

Thurloe
Sq

South Kensington
Station

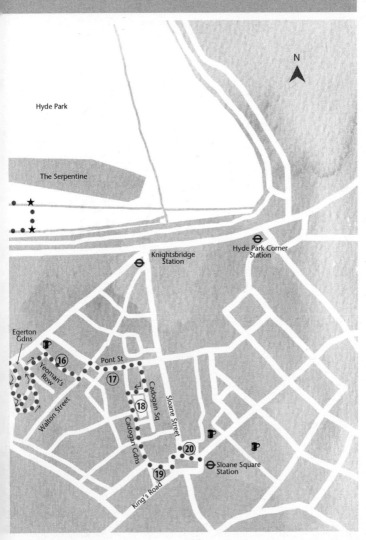

Hyde Park

The Serpentine

Hyde Park Corner
Station

Knightsbridge
Station

Egerton
Gdns

Yeoman's
Row

Walton Street

Pont St

Cadogan Sq

Sloane Street

Cadogan Gdns

King's Road

Sloane Square
Station

N

(16)
(17)
(18)
(19)
(20)

Chapter 1

Walking in Victorian South Kensington

We begin this leg of the walks at Kensington Palace, where Queen Victoria and the age to which she gave her name were born. We then explore the site of the Great Exhibition of 1851, the defining achievement of the Victorian Age, and the museum area of South Kensington, inspired by and financed out of the profits of that Exhibition. Here is perhaps the greatest accumulation of educational and cultural institutions anywhere in the world, and also some of London's most striking Victorian buildings. After Prince Albert, the driving force behind the Exhibition, died in 1861, buildings and memorials were erected in his memory overlooking the site of his greatest achievement and the area became known, affectionately, as Albertopolis.

Numbers applied to each attraction refer to the numbers on the map

Walks
Start walking: Queensway Station

☞ Exit the station, turn right into Queensway, cross Bayswater Road on your left then right and left into Kensington Gardens. Follow the Broad Walk to Kensington Palace.

(1)   # Kensington Palace
(1819 and 1837)

Kensington Palace is where the Victorian Age truly began. Not only was Victoria born here in 1819, but this is where she was in the early hours of 20 June 1837, at the moment that her uncle William IV died and she became queen. And it was at Kensington Palace, that same morning, that Victoria held her first Privy Council meeting, declaring, *'The severe and afflicting loss, which the nation has sustained by the death of his Majesty, my beloved uncle devolved upon me the duty of administering the government of this empire.'*

The Red Saloon where the meeting took place has been refurbished and laid out as it was for that occasion, and on the wall hangs a painting by Sir David Wilkie, that recreates the scene. To sit where Victoria sat, 18 years old, untested, surrounded by the 97 most powerful men in the land and yet showing *'perfect calmness and self-possession'*, is a moving experience.

No one knew it at the time, but that day in the Red Saloon marked the dawn of the modern world, and of the Victorian London that would become that new world's first city. The

Victorian Age would see London grow into the biggest, most populous, most prosperous and most famous city on Earth, the spiritual, political, financial and trading capital of the world and the beating heart of the biggest empire ever known. From London, Queen Victoria would rule over almost a quarter of the world's population and a fifth of the world's land mass.

Once you have visited Kensington Palace to see where Queen Victoria was born and the Red Saloon where she held her first Privy Council meeting, make your way to the statue of Queen Victoria that stands at the west entrance to the palace, gazing out over Kensington Gardens and the Round Pond. This was sculpted by Victoria's talented artist daughter Princess Louise in 1893.

H·R·H·PRINCESS LOUISE SCULP

☞ FROM THE STATUE GO TO THE ROUND POND AND WALK AROUND IT WITH THE POND ON YOUR LEFT. VEER

RIGHT AT THE FIRST PATH YOU COME TO, THEN LEFT ON TO
THE NEXT, BROADER, PATH. GO OVER TWO CROSSROADS
THEN RIGHT ON TO A BROADER PATH WHICH LEADS TO
THE ALBERT MEMORIAL.

② Albert Memorial
(1872)

When it was built the Albert Memorial was considered to be amongst the finest monuments in all Europe and today is seen as the epitome of High Victorian gothic grandeur, bold, ostentatious and oozing self-confidence. Commissioned by Queen Victoria as a national memorial to her beloved husband Albert, who died of typhoid in 1861 aged just 42, it was designed by Sir George Gilbert Scott and unveiled in 1872. A number of eminent architects competed for the commission, with Scott's design being chosen by the Queen herself, and Scott later received a knighthood for his work. The memorial, which is 175 feet (53 m) high and contains huge quantities of marble, enamels, bronze and mosaics, cost £10 million in today's money and the Prime Minister of the day William Gladstone attempted to delay the project on the grounds of cost, a move which did not improve his already strained relations with the Queen.

At the four outer corners of the memorial are groups of marble statues illustrating Africa, the Americas, Asia and Europe, featuring suitably ethnic characters and a representative animal, a camel, a bison, an elephant and a bull, respectively, while at the four corners of the podium are groups symbolic of Agriculture, Commerce, Manufacturing and Engineering. The white marble

Frieze of Parnassus around the base of the podium consists of 187 life-size statues of painters (on the east side), poets and musicians (on the south side), architects (on the north side) and sculptors (on the west side), the latter two being arranged in chronological order. A shiny new pound coin for anyone who can find Sir George Gilbert Scott himself amongst the architects. There are further statues on the pillars and in niches in the canopy, all of them watched over by eight gilt bronzed angels.

The 14 foot (4.3 m) high gilt bronze statue of Prince Albert is by John Foley and was put in place in 1876. The Prince is seated and holds in his right hand a catalogue of the Great Exhibition of 1851.

☞ NOW GO DOWN THE STEPS IN FRONT OF THE MEMORIAL AND TURN LEFT ONTO THE BROAD TARMAC CARRIAGEWAY. WALK TO THE GATES AT THE END.

③ Coalbrookdale Gates
(c.1850)

These cast-iron gates are virtually the only surviving structure from the Great Exhibition that remains in the park where the Exhibition was held. They stood at the entrance to the north transept of the Crystal Palace and were cast at Coalbrookdale in Shropshire by the pioneering Coalbrookdale Company, the first and largest iron foundry in the world, and builders of the world's first iron bridge. Written along the base of the gates are the words 'Cast in Coalbrookdale' – it's spine-tingling to think that they are a product of the workshop that triggered the Industrial Revolution.

☞ NOW CROSS THE ROAD IN FRONT OF YOU, WEST CARRIAGE DRIVE, AND GO STRAIGHT AHEAD ON THE TREE-

LINED PATH ALONGSIDE SOUTH CARRIAGE DRIVE. JUST
AFTER THE PRINCE OF WALES GATE THERE IS A PLAQUE
TO THE LEFT OF THE PATH SHOWING THE LOCATION OF
THE CRYSTAL PALACE WITHIN HYDE PARK.

(4) Site of the Crystal Palace
(1851)

The Crystal Palace was built to house the world's first international exhibition of manufactured goods, the Great Exhibition of 1851, organised by Prince Albert and Henry Cole as a showcase for contemporary industrial design and technology from all over the world. The exhibition hosted some 14,000 exhibitors showing over 100,000 exhibits, lasted just over five months and was visited by six million people, the equivalent of a third of the population of Victorian Britain at that time. As well as the Royal Family, famous visitors included Charlotte Brontë, Charles Dickens, Charles Darwin, Lewis Carroll, George Eliot and Alfred Lord Tennyson. Profits from the exhibition, £186,000, or £16 million in today's money, were used to fund the Victoria and Albert Museum, the Science Museum and the Natural History Museum.

The Crystal Palace itself was designed by Joseph Paxton from a concept sketched on a piece of pink blotting paper, which can be seen in the Victoria and Albert Museum. A vast structure of cast iron and glass, it was inspired by the famous Great Conservatory at Chatsworth House, which Paxton had designed and built for the 6th Duke of Devonshire. The Crystal Palace, not only the largest building made of glass the world had ever seen but the largest building in the world at the time, was

1,848 feet (563 m) long and 408 feet (124 m) wide and enclosed an area of 23 acres (9.3 ha). As you stand at the plaque looking north you are standing at what was the entrance to the barrel-vaulted central transept, which was raised to a height of 108 feet (33 m) to accommodate a number of living elm trees.

After the exhibition the Crystal Palace was taken down and rebuilt in Sydenham, where it burned down in 1936. There is almost nothing left of it in Hyde Park, although some of the concrete platform on which it rested remains under the grass playing fields, and in 2016 the remains of a brick-lined earth closet built as a public loo for visitors to the exhibition were discovered near the tennis centre. A highlight of the exhibition was the introduction of the world's first paid-for flushing public lavatories, invented by a Brighton plumber called George Jennings. The charge was one penny – hence the expression spend a penny. Jennings persuaded Henry Cole to keep the lavatories open for some years after the Exhibition closed and the idea gained popularity with growing numbers of 'Public Retiring Rooms' springing up throughout London, many of them built by the prolific Sir Samuel Morton Peto, builder amongst many other places of Nelson's Column and the Reform Club, who we come across several times on our walks.

Optional marker walk

The location of the four corners of the Crystal Palace are marked by round plaques set into the pavement, and by walking to each of these plaques you can get a sense of the enormous scale of the structure. From the plaque by the Prince of Wales Gate continue east along the tree-lined path and you will find the south-east corner plaque about 100 yards (90 m) beyond the tower of Knightsbridge Barracks looming on the other side of the road. From here turn left and cut due north across the playing fields to find the north-east plaque. From there turn left and go west along the path with the playing fields on your left and you will find the north-west plaque set into the path just as it begins to curve around past the tennis courts. Continue on the path as it bears left past the bowling green and you will find the south-west plaque right outside the Pavilion café.

☞ From the café make your way back to the Coalbrookdale Gates by crossing West Carriage Drive. Turn left in front of the gates, then cross Kensington Road and turn right. On your left is Lowther Lodge.

⑤ Lowther Lodge – Royal Geographical Society
(1873)

Lowther Lodge was designed by Norman Shaw in 1873 as a private house for William Lowther MP, and was Shaw's first large commission in London. Shaw made the Queen Anne style very much his own and would become perhaps the foremost domestic architect of the later Victorian period. Lowther Lodge was not just innovative in its architecture but was also at the cutting edge of the new technology – it was the first private house in London to have a lift, which is still in use in the main hall. Lowther Lodge remained a private house until 1912 when it was sold by the Lowther family to the Royal Geographical Society for its headquarters.

☞ Continue west along Kensington Gore.

⑥ Albert Hall Mansions
(1880)

Towering over Lowther Lodge to the west is Albert Hall Mansions, London's first mansion block, designed in a red-brick, Flemish style by Norman Shaw in 1880 with little regard to how the vast new edifice would overpower his earlier, rather more elegant work at Lowther Lodge. By the late nineteenth century London's population was exploding, and building land in the west of the city was becoming scarce. Even the wealthy had to learn to squeeze into apartment blocks, previously the preserve of the working classes. To make the idea more palatable, fashionable architects were hired to design grand 'mansion' blocks that resembled hotels, with spacious lobbies and uniformed doormen. The apartments were sumptuous, with wine cellars, bathrooms, accommodation for staff, balconies with iron railings and the latest technology, such as lifts. Albert Hall Mansions set the benchmark for apartment blocks all over London and the style was copied for the next 30 years. Look for the neat little oriel windows beneath the Dutch gables on the fifth floor – they were a favourite embellishment of Shaw's.

☞ CONTINUE ALONG KENSINGTON GORE.

⑦ Royal Albert Hall
(1867–71)

Queen Victoria laid the foundation stone of the Central Hall of Arts and Sciences in 1867, declaring that it should henceforth be known as the Royal Albert Hall of Arts and Sciences in memory of her husband, Prince Albert. That very

foundation stone can still be seen, beneath seat 87 in row 11 of the K stalls.

In response to Prince Albert's suggestion that the profits from the Great Exhibition of 1851 be used to establish a permanent centre for the arts and sciences, the Royal Commission in charge of the Exhibition's finances purchased a parcel of land on the south edge of Hyde Park on which to build the facilities. The area was centred on Gore House, the easternmost house of a row of large mansions that had been built alongside the road from Kensington to London in the eighteenth century. In 1850, after it had been purchased by the Commission, Gore House became Soyer's Gastronomic Symposium of All Nations, a fashionable restaurant catering for visitors to the Great Exhibition run by French chef Alexis Soyer, formerly of the Reform Club (*see* page 245).

In 1857 Gore House was demolished and work began on the Royal Albert Hall, designed by Captain Francis Fowke and

Colonel H.Y. Darracott Scott of the Royal Engineers, was erected on the site, being completed in 1871. Hailed for being as grand and imposing as anything from the glory days of Rome it was built to resemble an amphitheatre, it is elliptical in shape, 740 feet (225m) in circumference, with a central dome of glass and steel 135 feet (41m) high, and can accommodate some 7000 people. The frieze that runs around the outside of the building illustrates the Triumph of Art and Letters.

The Hall's first concert, performed to test the acoustics, was held on 25 February 1871 when an amateur orchestra, The Wandering Minstrels, played in front of an invited audience that included the men who had worked on the building and their families. In fact the acoustics turned out to be dire, with a notorious echo that gave rise to the quip that *'the only place where a British composer could be sure of hearing his work twice is the Albert Hall'*. It wasn't until 1968 that the problem was solved by suspending sound absorbent discs from the dome.

On 29 March 1871 the Royal Albert Hall was officially declared open by Edward, Prince of Wales, with the words, *'The Queen declares this Hall is now open'*, the Queen herself being too overcome with emotion to speak. Highlights at the Hall during the Victorian Age included the Great Wagner Festival in 1877, with the orchestra conducted by Richard Wagner himself, Sunday afternoon concerts with the likes of Dame Nellie Melba and Adelina Patti, and a talk in 1890 by Sir Henry Morton Stanley about his travels in Africa searching for David Livingstone. In 1891 the Hall hosted the world's first ever sci-fi convention, an event inspired by the hugely popular science fiction novel by Lord Lytton, *Vril: The Power of the Coming Race*. The Hall was dressed up to look like Vril-ya, a city inhabited by winged super beings, represented by mannequins flying overhead. There were Vril themed magic shows and entertainments and even stalls selling mugs of Bovril, whose name was derived from the words 'Bovine' and 'Vril'.

Now walk anti-clockwise round the Royal Albert Hall to the south side, passing through an area of dark and echoing canyons created by the giant red-brick mansion blocks that wrap around the Hall. This spot is pure Victoriana.

(8) Memorial to the Exhibition of 1851
(1863)

At the top of the steps leading down to Prince Consort Road is a monument that should be better known but, because of its location tucked away behind the Royal Albert Hall, goes largely un-remarked. The Memorial to the Exhibition of 1851 was designed by Joseph Durham with help from Sydney Smirke and is made from two varieties of granite, Aberdeen Red and Cornish. Four bronze female figures sit at the base of the pedestal representing Europe, America, Asia and Africa, while Prince Albert stands on top gazing out over Albertopolis. The original plan was to have a statue of Britannia at the top, but after Prince Albert's death Queen Victoria requested that it should be a statue of Albert, as one of the two main driving forces behind the Exhibition. The memorial was eventually erected in 1863 in the show gardens of the Royal Horticultural Society nearby, but was moved to its present site in 1891 when the gardens were demolished to make way for Prince Consort Road.

⑨ Royal College of Organists
(1875)

A little further round the Hall, on the west side, is one of the most memorable houses in London, the extraordinary Royal College of Organists, recognisable to many as the home of Mr Selfridge in the ITV drama series of that name. It was built as the National Training School for Music in 1875 and designed by Lieutenant H.H. Cole, the eldest son of Henry Cole, the other main driving force behind the Great Exhibition. The entire façade of the house, except for the large windows, is covered in decorative raised plasterwork known as sgraffito, while a frieze depicting a variety of musicians runs above the front door and ground-floor windows. The National Training School for Music was soon replaced by

27

the Royal College of Music, and in 1904 the Royal College of Organists moved in. They moved on in 1990 but left their name behind.

(10) Royal College of Music
(1890–4)

Framing Prince Albert's view from his Exhibition Memorial is the vast Gothic Royal College of Music, designed by Sir Arthur Blomfield, in a kind of grand Baronial style that might be considered overpowering, but it is certainly not uninteresting. There may be a touch of Dracula's castle about it, but it makes an impressive statement, and had the building been there when Wagner was conducting in the Albert Hall it might have inspired that redoubtable composer to even darker dramatic heights. The foundation stone was laid in 1890 to the accompaniment of some lustily performed music belted out by the Leeds Forge Brass Band brought along by Samson Fox, the Yorkshire industrialist who financed the building, and whose bust stands in the entrance hall. Samson Fox was responsible for one of the most significant inventions of the Victorian Age, the corrugated boiler flue, which enabled small boilers to work under much greater pressure than had previously been the case. He was also patriarch of the Fox acting dynasty, being great-grandfather to Edward and James Fox and great-great-grandfather to Emilia and Laurence Fox.

Now go down the steps into Prince Consort Road and look back towards the Albert Hall for a glorious vista of Victorian red and white, quite unlike any other view in London. With the Royal College of Music at your back, turn to your right and proceed along Prince Consort Road. Albert Court, the apartment block on the left, was built between 1890 and 1889. You will notice that the top floors are rather plain compared to the elaborate lower floors. The building had reached the fourth floor when the builders ran out of money and the top three floors, above what became known as the 'bankruptcy line', had to be completed as cheaply as possible.

The red-brick house with terracotta decoration on the corner as you reach Exhibition Road is one of a pair of attractive Queen Anne style houses built in 1876 by J.J. Stevenson. It now houses the Jamaican High Commission.

Turn right into Exhibition Road, go past the ultra-modern Imperial College building and turn right into Imperial College Road until you come to a tall Renaissance style tower, standing at the front of an open square and looking somewhat out of keeping with the modernity surrounding it. The whole area between Prince Consort Road and Imperial College Road was at one time occupied by the Imperial Institute, founded after the Colonial Exhibition of 1886. It was housed in a huge stone building designed by Thomas Collcutt and constructed between 1886 and 1893. This building was demolished bit by bit from 1957 onwards and replaced over time by the present modern blocks of Imperial College, leaving just this one tower from the original Victorian complex.

(11) The Queen's Tower
(1887)

At 287 feet (87 m) high, the Queen's Tower is the tallest structure in this part of Kensington, and yet still comes

as a surprise, tucked away as it is down a private gated road and hidden from view by the encircling Imperial College buildings. In fact the tower's distinctive copper dome can be glimpsed from Kensington Gardens if you know where to look. The Queen's Tower was the central one of the Imperial Institute's three towers, and was only saved from being demolished along with the rest of the Institute in the 1960s thanks to a fiercely fought campaign of local enthusiasts ably abetted by Sir John Betjeman. The foundations and base had to be reinforced so that the tower could become free-standing.

Built to mark Queen Victoria's Golden Jubilee, the tower contains a set of ten bells named after Victoria and some of her children and grandchildren, which are still rung on royal anniversaries. A series of spiral staircases consisting of 325 steps lead up to a viewing gallery at the base of the dome, from where there are stupendous views over London in all directions. The gallery used to be open to the public, and hopefully will be again one day, but for now the views can only be enjoyed by special arrangement with Imperial College. The entrance to the tower is guarded by two stone lions from a set of four that once sat at the entrance to the Imperial Institute.

☞ NOW RETURN TO EXHIBITION ROAD AND TURN RIGHT.

(12) Henry Cole Wing
(1868–73)

On the left after 100 yards (90 m), and hard to miss, is the monumental red-brick and terracotta Henry Cole Wing of the Victoria and Albert Museum, named in honour of the museum's first director. It was constructed between 1868 and 1873, with Henry Cole himself having a hand in the design, along with Henry Scott and Richard Redgrave. Many of the Early Renaissance style decorative features on the building such as the mosaics, the moulded terracotta, the putti and other figures on the pillars were a first for a Victorian building and something of an experiment. Note, also, the open loggia on the top storey. Inside, the Grand Staircase is particularly impressive. The building was first occupied by the School of Naval Architects, then the Science School and finally Imperial College, before being annexed to the V&A in 1978. The stone screen in front of the newly paved area next to the Henry Cole Wing was put up in 1909 by Aston Webb to hide the unsightly boiler house yard that was located there originally The stonework of the screen still shows signs of the bomb damage it suffered during the Second World War.

Victoria and Albert Museum
(1857 onwards)

At the end of Exhibition Road, turn left for the Victoria and Albert Museum. Pause outside the main entrance, a monumental edifice designed by Aston Webb, with a tower above the door 185 feet (56 m) high and shaped at the top like an Imperial crown. Queen Victoria laid the foundation stone in 1899, her last major public engagement, and it was on this occasion that the museum, known as the South Kensington Museum when it opened here in 1857, was renamed the Victoria and Albert Museum. That foundation stone can be seen to the left of the main entrance door.

Before you go into the museum, look back across the road and a little to the left. Facing the museum, from the end of a terrace, is a Victorian house nestling behind a tree and a red pillar box. This is No. 33 Thurloe Square, the former home of Sir Henry Cole (1808–1882), Commissioner for the Great Exhibition and first director of the Victoria and Albert Museum, who in his spare time designed the world's first adhesive postage stamp, the Penny Black, and invented the Christmas card.

The Victoria and Albert Museum was founded in 1852 as the Museum of Manufactures, and amongst its first collections were many of the products exhibited at the Great Exhibition. The museum opened initially in Marlborough House and then moved in with the School of Design at Somerset House until, in 1857, Henry Cole organised the transfer of all the exhibits of both museum and school to South Kensington, where they were temporarily housed in a huge glass and corrugated iron shed described by *The Builder* magazine as looking 'like a threefold

Sir Henry Cole

monster boiler'. Despite Prince Albert's attempts to prettify the structure by having it painted with green and white stripes, the shed became known as the Brompton Boilers, and in the 1860s it was removed to Bethnal Green where it was re-erected, clad with new brick walls, to house what became the Victoria and Albert Museum of Childhood.

In the meantime new museum buildings were being put up in South Kensington, many of which are now hidden away behind the later Aston Webb frontage. Some have been remodelled over the years and rendered pretty much unrecognisable, although they still form the core of the museum complex. The oldest building is the Sheepshanks Gallery, which was built in 1857 by Captain Fowke (who later built the Albert Hall) to house a picture collection donated by Yorkshire manufacturer John Sheepshanks. This extended north from the Brompton Boilers and, although much altered, survives today as Rooms 26, 29, 84, 92 and 93.

In 1858 Fowke added two more galleries stretching north and east to house the National Gallery's Turner and Vernon collections. These form the north-east section of the museum, now Rooms 81, 82, 87, 88, 88a and 94. In 1861 the Eastern Galleries completed the eastern side of the square formed by the new buildings. This is now Rooms 96 to 101 on Level 3 with offices below.

In 1863 Fowke roofed over the quadrangle formed by the 'Boilers' and the new galleries and divided the space into two to make the North and South Courts, now used as galleries for temporary exhibitions.

The Italian Renaissance style buildings and pavilions that enclose what is now the John Madejski Garden to the north, west and east were designed and begun by Fowke in 1863 and finished off in 1869 by Henry Scott, with external decoration by Geoffrey Sykes. The wonderful Lecture Theatre building on the north side, with the three recessed arches, was originally intended as the main entrance to the museum, and before the Aston Webb building was completed in the early

1900s, it faced south to the Cromwell Road across an area of grass. The splendid bronze front door is sculpted with figures from the history of the arts and sciences, while inscribed above it is the typically Victorian maxim, '*Better it is to get wisdom than gold*'.

While you are in the courtyard look out for two plaques set into the wall of the Madejski Garden. They both commemorate dogs, Henry Cole's faithful Yorkshire terrier Jim (who appeared with his master in a cartoon in *Vanity Fair* in 1871) and Tycho, who belonged to Henry's son Alan Cole.

Inside, off the Silver Galleries on Level 3, is the much restored Victorian lecture theatre, while just inside the bronze doors on the ground floor is the world's first museum restaurant, made up of three glorious interlinked Refreshment Rooms, the Gamble, Poynter and Morris Rooms. The V&A was the first museum in the world to offer Refreshment Rooms on the premises, the original rooms being housed in a mock-Tudor building that stood to the east of the 'Boilers', close to where Brompton Oratory is now.

The Gamble Room, built between 1865 and 1878 and originally known as the Centre Refreshment Room, was the first room that visitors entering by the original entrance would have seen and it must have made quite an impression. Ornate enamelled iron plates, similar to the name plates on railway stations, adorn the ceiling, while the walls and columns are covered with ceramic tiles, all designed to be fireproof and easily washable. The stained-glass windows are emblazoned with sayings about the joys of eating and drinking, and the frieze running around the window columns shows a quotation from Ecclesiastes 2:24, '*There is nothing better for a man than that he should eat and drink, and make his soul enjoy the good of his labour.'*

To the west of the Gamble Room (on the left as you enter) is the Morris Room, or Green Dining Room, decorated from 1867 onwards by William Morris's company, their first major commission. The panels and stained-glass windows are by Edward Burne-Jones and much of the decoration by Philip Webb, while the influence of Morris himself can be seen in the berries, leaves and flowers of the plasterwork.

To the east (on the right as you enter) is the Grill Room, or Poynter Room, furnished with tiled wooden panelling and Dutch blue tiles designed by Edward Poynter. The tiled panels depicting the four seasons and the 12 months were painted by students from a special ladies' tile-painting class set up at the Schools of Design, a radical idea in the 1860s but typical of Henry Cole, whose aim was to involve as many people as possible in the creation of his museum. There is a fashionable Japanese influence at work here too, shown in the flowers on the blue tiles, the peacocks on the frieze and the wave patterns on the doors of the huge iron stove, still in place against the wall.

In each of these Refreshment Rooms visitors can sample a selection of Victorian dishes, as well as more modern fare, and there is nowhere better in London in which to enjoy an authentic Victorian refreshment experience, hence I have included the V&A Refreshment Rooms in the list of recommended Places for Refreshment on this walk.

Another highlight of this part of the museum is the Ceramic or West Staircase, now romantically named Staircase 1. This was created between 1864 and 1868 by a master of the School of Design, Frank Moody, with the help of his students, using terracotta and mosaics for the walls and steps. The barrel-vaulted ceilings are decorated with ceramic paintings.

Since its foundation the Victoria and Albert Museum has absorbed collections and treasures from every aspect of art and design from all over the world almost at random, and it is now the largest museum of decorative arts and design in the world. It was also, incidentally, the first museum in the world to be lit, initially by gas lamps, as Henry Cole was keen that working people should be able to visit the museum in the evening after working hours.

☞ EXIT THE V&A AND TURN RIGHT FOR THE NATURAL HISTORY MUSEUM, ONE OF THE GREAT VICTORIAN PALACES OF LONDON, ON THE OTHER SIDE OF EXHIBITION ROAD.

(14) Natural History Museum
(1881)

Sir Richard Owen, the first Superintendent of the Natural History Department of the British Museum, which became the Natural History Museum, and the man who invented the term 'dinosaur', wanted his museum to be a *'cathedral to nature'*. His architect, Alfred Waterhouse, certainly did him proud. Opened in 1881, the Natural History Museum was Waterhouse's first public building in London. A vast Flemish Romanesque extravaganza, sheathed inside and out in hard-wearing terracotta, the building quickly became a striking London landmark. The front is 675 feet (206 m) long, and the twin towers over the entrance door are 192 feet (59 m) high. The cathedral-like

Central Hall (now the Hintze Hall) is spectacular, with a roof of glass and steel and a grand staircase at the far end from the entrance. The idea was for a space big enough to display the skeletons of the world's largest creatures, the first such creature being a sperm whale, which was installed in the 1890s. As well as the exhibits, the whole museum is decorated with ornaments, statues, relief sculptures and carvings inspired by nature, many of them designed by Waterhouse himself. Owen stipulated that these depictions of creatures, flora and fauna should be divided into two halves, with the extinct in the east wing and the living in the west wing so as to make it more difficult to link the past and the present as Darwin was at the time attempting with his Theory of Evolution. Missed by many visitors, understandably, are the beautiful tiles showing flowers and plants from across the world that adorn the ceilings of the galleries – as so often in London, it is well worth looking up.

☞ EXIT THE MUSEUM AND TURN LEFT. GO BACK PAST THE VICTORIA AND ALBERT MUSEUM TO THE BROMPTON ORATORY.

(15) Brompton Oratory
(1884)

Just past the museum, on a wall inside the Oratory grounds, there is a marble statue of Cardinal Newman (1801–1890), sculpted by Léon-Joseph Chavalliaud in 1896. Newman was a former Anglican priest who was received into the Catholic Church in 1845 and founded the first Oratory in Britain in Birmingham in 1849. This was a community of Catholic priests dedicated to the teachings of St Philip Neri, a priest in sixteenth-century Rome. The London Oratory followed swiftly and their Oratory House can be seen on the far side of the courtyard beyond the statue. It was built in 1853 and designed in quiet Italian Renaissance style by Joseph Scoles, architect of the Church of the Immaculate Conception in Farm Street (*see* page 239). Next to it is the great Church of the Immaculate Heart of Mary, otherwise known as the Brompton Oratory, designed by Herbert Gribble and consecrated in 1884. Everything about the church is designed to create the feeling of being in Italy. The building is a mix of Italian Renaissance and Roman Baroque and is based on the mother church of the Congregation of the Oratory, the Church of Chiesa Nuova in Rome. It is faced with Portland stone and sports a 200 foot (61 m) high dome and cupola. The glorious interior is rich Italian Baroque with a wide nave and side chapels, numerous altars with decoration by Italian artists, painted domes, Romanesque arches, marble columns and giant marble statues of the Apostles from Siena Cathedral. Until Westminster Cathedral opened in 1903, Brompton Oratory was the largest Catholic church in London and hosted all the big Catholic ceremonies in London including the funeral of Cardinal Manning in 1892.

☞ EXIT BROMPTON ORATORY AND GO STRAIGHT ACROSS THE ROAD INTO EGERTON GARDENS. TURN RIGHT AND FOLLOW EGERTON GARDENS AS IT CURVES LEFT.

The houses in Egerton Gardens were put up between 1886 and 1895 and were designed by a variety of architects, mainly in Queen Anne style.

At the end of Egerton Gardens turn right. Mortimer House, a large detached house with a big private garden on your right, was built in 1886–8 for Edward Palmer, a former governor of the Bank of England, and is still privately owned. It is mix of Tudor and Jacobean styles, red-brick with blue-brick patternwork, stone mullioned windows, Tudor chimneys and Jacobean gables, and looks amazingly authentic. It also comes as a bit of a (pleasant) surprise amongst the standard Victorian terraces of South Kensington. Now turn left into Egerton Crescent, often described as *'the most expensive street in Britain'*. This was built in the early 1840s by local builder James Bonnin and designed by George Basevi, the architect of the Smith's Charity Estate, a large local landowner. Walk along the crescent and at the end turn right into Egerton Gardens. Follow the road round to the left, in front of Egerton Place, built in 1886, and then turn right through the brick gateposts into Egerton Gardens Mews.

Yeoman's Row
(1880–90)

Go to the end and into Yeoman's Row. If you require refreshment turn left for the early Victorian Bunch of Grapes pub, otherwise turn right. The west (right-hand) side of Yeoman's Row is lined with stables and mews houses built for Egerton Place in the 1880s and 1890s. Nos. 6–10 in yellow brick were stables, with accommodation for grooms on the first floor. Then comes a row of artist's studios, hence the big windows, built in 1898. No. 22 was designed by Alfred Beesley and also built in 1898, as the roundels below the first-floor window tell us. Nos. 24, 26 and 28 were all designed by William Barber in different styles for three lady artists in 1898–9.

☞ Go to the end of the row and then through the narrow passageway into Walton Street, which was laid out in 1847.

Facing you, across the road, is the Old Magistrates' Court, built as a school around 1850 – note the separate entrances for Girls and Boys in the main street and the iron bars on the windows looking out on to the side street beside the building.

☞ Turn left on Walton Street and continue past Lennox Gardens on the right, full of Queen Anne style houses built between 1882 and 1886, and then turn left at the lights into Pont Street.

Pont Street
(1870s)

Pont Street is lined with red-brick houses built in the late 1870s in a distinctive Queen Anne style that became known as Pont Street Dutch, no doubt due to the profusion of variously shaped Dutch gables that decorate the skyline. Many of these houses are the work of J.J. Stevenson. Although Norman Shaw is the architect most famously associated with the Queen Anne style, which is defined by red brick, white-painted windows, terracotta mouldings, asymmetrical appearance at ground-floor level and, most prominently, gables, Stevenson can claim to have invented it for his own house, the Red House in Bayswater Road, built in 1871 but since demolished. Stevenson described the style as Free Classical and thought it much suited to domestic property since it was free from the religious connotations of the Gothic and the foreign influence of the Classical. The Queen Anne style certainly proved popular in this part of London, where acres of Pont Street Dutch houses, terraces and mansion blocks sprang up over the next two decades.

Cadogan Square
(1870s and 1880s)

Take the third turning right for the east side of Cadogan Square, most of which was built in 1879 by G.T. Robinson. No. 4 on the north-east corner of the square comes as a surprise, being Gothic amongst the Queen Anne. It was designed by G.E. Street, architect of the Royal Courts of Justice, for the Bishop of Gloucester, hence the church elements. Turn right in front of No. 4 and walk along the north side of the square, mostly the work of G.T. Robinson. Then turn left and walk down the west side. No. 50, very distinctive in pale red brick, was designed in 1887 by Sir Ernest George for Sir Thomas De La Rue, chairman of the printing firm, while next door, Nos. 54–58, Pont Street Dutch with Renaissance details, was built by William Young for Lord Cadogan in 1890. No. 62 on the corner of Milner Street was built by Norman Shaw in 1883. Nos. 68 and 72, both built in 1877, are instantly recognisable as Shaw's work with his distinctive tall rectangular small-paned windows and deliberate lack of symmetry. Nos. 63–73 on the south side of the square were designed by J.J. Stevenson in 1885–6 and are reminiscent of his Pont Street work. Stevenson's desire to make each house in the terrace different can sometimes, as here, result in something of a befuddled look.

(19) No. 25 Cadogan Gardens
(1883)

☞ LEAVE THE SQUARE ALONG THE WEST SIDE AND
AT THE MINI ROUNDABOUT GO STRAIGHT OVER INTO
CADOGAN GARDENS. WALK ALMOST TO THE END PAST
DRAYCOTT PLACE, ON THE RIGHT, AND THE CONCRETE
TRIANGLE FORMED BY SYMONS STREET ON THE LEFT.

In front of you is No. 25, red brick with tall rectangular windows and the number displayed prominently on the wall. This was built in 1894 as a studio home for a friend of J.M. Whistler, the Australian-born artist Mortimer Menpes. The architect was Arthur Heygate Mackmurdo, whose swirling foliage design for the cover of his own book *Wren's City Churches*, published in 1883, has been described as the first example of Art Nouveau design. You can recognise Mackmurdo's work by the slender square columns with flat square tops framing the front door, a design unique to Mackmurdo. Note also that the north-facing windows are oriel windows and much more lavish than the west-facing windows, reflecting the importance of the north light to artists. The interior was decorated in Japanese style with carved panelling made in Japan and rooms full of Japanese ornaments, statues, vases and furniture, and the house was described by the silent movie actor Raymond Blathwayt as *'the most wonderful house in the world. To wander through its entrance hall is as though one walked in a garden of the far Eastern world …'* When Menpes sold the house in 1907, all the furniture was auctioned off and the house itself is now owned by Peter Jones, the large department store that backs on to it.

 NOW TURN LEFT AND WALK DOWN SYMONS STREET INTO SLOANE SQUARE. CROSS SLOANE STREET USING THE PEDESTRIAN CROSSING AND TURN LEFT FOR HOLY TRINITY CHURCH.

(20) Holy Trinity, Sloane Square
(1890)

Holy Trinity, which was designed by John Dando Sedding in 1888 and completed after his death by his assistant Henry Wilson in 1890, was described by Sir John Betjeman as the '*Cathedral of the Arts & Crafts Movement*'. The interior is full of superb sculptures by leading 'New Sculptors' – Frederick

Pomeroy designed the choir, Henry Armstead, the nave and lectern, and Onslow Ford, the font. The wonderful east window, big and colourful, was designed by Edward Burne-Jones and executed by William Morris & Co.

☞ ON LEAVING THE CHURCH TURN LEFT FOR SLOANE SQUARE STATION AND THE ANTELOPE AND DUKE OF WELLINGTON PUBS.

End of walks: Sloane Square Station

Recommended Places for Refreshment

Any of the Refreshment Rooms at the V&A

The Bunch of Grapes 207 Brompton Road, SW3 (corner of Yeoman's Row)

The Antelope 22 Eaton Terrace, SW1 (just off Sloane Square)

The Duke of Wellington 63 Eaton Terrace, SW1 (just off Sloane Square)

N

Ilchester Pl

Holland Park

Phillimore Gdns

Argyll Rd

Stafford Terrace
①

Kensington High Street

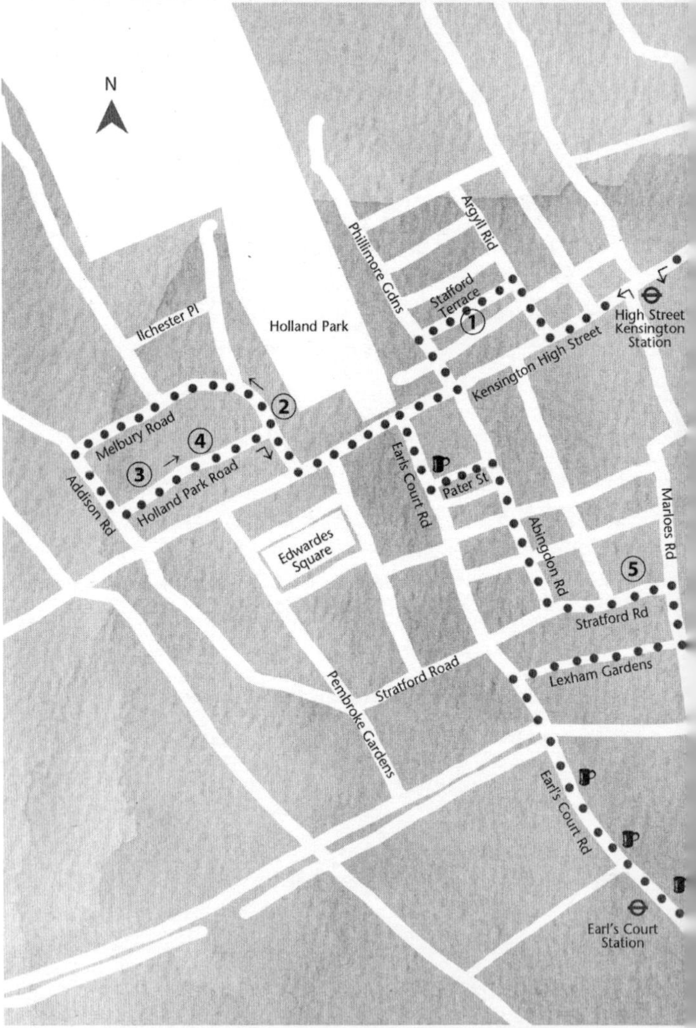

High Street
Kensington
Station

Melbury Road
④
②
③ →
Holland Park Road

Addison Rd

Earls Court Rd

Pater St

Abingdon Rd

Marloes Rd

Edwardes
Square

⑤
Stratford Rd

Stratford Road

Lexham Gardens

Pembroke Gardens

Earl's Court Rd

Earl's Court
Station

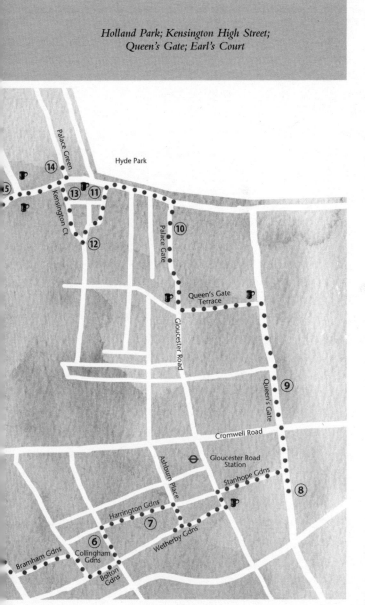

Hyde Park

Palace Green

Kensington Ct.

Palace Gate

Gloucester Road

Queen's Gate Terrace

Queen's Gate

Cromwell Road

Gloucester Road Station

Ashburn Place

Stanhope Gdns

Harrington Gdns

Wetherby Gdns

Bramham Gdns

Collingham Gdns

Bolton Gdns

Chapter 2
Walking in Victorian Kensington

O n this part of the walks we explore the many faces of
Kensington, an area sometimes described as a 'Victorian
Citadel' containing, as it does, numerous outstanding examples
of Victorian architecture and miles of residential streets lined
with smart Victorian villas and gardens. Formerly a village
straddling one of the two major roads out of London to the
west and notable mainly for market gardening and one or two
large country houses, Kensington became fashionable when
William III bought one of those country houses, Nottingham
House, in 1689 and turned it into Kensington Palace. Kensington
then became accessible when the railway arrived in 1868, and
became bohemian when the Great Exhibition of 1851, held in
Hyde Park, drew artists to the area.

Numbers applied to each attraction refer to the numbers on the map

Walks

Start walking: High Street Kensington Station

The walking begins at High Street Kensington Station, which was opened in 1868 as Kensington Station. If arriving by train, as you exit through the barriers and emerge into the octagonal hall where the station booking office was once located, turn and look back at the archway leading from the station. On the wall above you can see the initials of the railway companies that served the station in Victorian times, MR for Metropolitan Railway and DR for District Railway.

☞ EXIT THE STATION AND TURN LEFT ALONG KENSINGTON HIGH STREET. CROSS THE HIGH STREET AT THE FIRST LIGHTS AND TURN LEFT. CONTINUE ALONG THE HIGH STREET AND TAKE THE SECOND RIGHT INTO ARGYLL ROAD. TAKE THE SECOND LEFT INTO STAFFORD TERRACE AND ON THE LEFT AT NO. 18 IS THE HOUSE OF LINLEY SAMBOURNE.

① No. 18 Stafford Terrace (Linley Sambourne House)
(1874)

Edward Linley Sambourne, illustrator and cartoonist for *Punch* magazine, lived in this Victorian town house from 1874 until his death in 1910. The house was fairly newly built when Sambourne moved in and he set about decorating it in the Aesthetic style that was popular at the time, filling the rooms with exotic Middle Eastern and Oriental ornaments and furniture. Throughout the house there are numerous examples of Chinese porcelain and Japanese artworks, as well as stained-glass windows and William Morris wallpaper. There are also works by some of the leading illustrators of the day, including Kate Greenaway, the children's book illustrator and writer, and fellow *Punch* cartoonists George du Maurier and John Tenniel, the latter famous for his illustrations of *Alice's Adventures in Wonderland* and other Lewis Carroll books.

Sambourne's children preserved the house almost exactly as their father left it, so that today it provides a unique example of a late Victorian middle-class terraced home. Sambourne's granddaughter Anne, Countess of Rosse, was so enchanted by the house and its contents that she was inspired to found a society to fight for the preservation of Victorian buildings and artworks everywhere. The very first meeting of the Victorian Society was held in Linley Sambourne's house in 1958. Amongst the founding members present were John Betjeman and Nikolaus Pevsner.

☞ ON EXITING LINLEY SAMBOURNE HOUSE TURN LEFT AND GO TO THE END OF STAFFORD TERRACE. TURN LEFT INTO PHILLIMORE GARDENS AND AT THE END TURN RIGHT INTO KENSINGTON HIGH STREET. GO PAST THE ENTRANCE TO HOLLAND PARK AND THEN THE DESIGN MUSEUM AND TAKE THE NEXT RIGHT INTO MELBURY ROAD.

② **Melbury Road**
(c.1875)

Melbury Road, named after the Dorset country home of the Earls of Ilchester, was laid out in 1875 in the grounds of the Earl's Little Holland House, which had been demolished in 1871. The artist G.F. Watts, who had been living in Little Holland House with his wife the actress Ellen Terry, built himself a studio on the new road, starting a trend for other artists to do the same. Hence Melbury Road became the centre of a Victorian artist's colony, home to a group known as the Holland Park Circle. Watt's studio was demolished in the 1960s and replaced by a block of flats, Kingfisher House, but many of the other studio homes have survived, and Melbury Road and the surrounding streets retain a distinctive arty atmosphere.

☞ NOW WALK ON UP MELBURY ROAD.

Nos. 57 and 55 on the right were designed by Halsey Ricardo and built in 1894, originally as a pair of semi-detached houses. Ricardo chose to use dark red glazed brick for these houses as protection against the polluted London air. The first occupant of No. 57 was Sir Ernest Debenham, who later employed Ricardo to design an exotic house for him in nearby Addison Road.

No. 47, also on the right, was built in 1893 and designed by Dudley Oliver as a studio home for the artist Walford Robertson, who lived there with Scottish impressionist painter Arthur Melville. The house was added to in 1912. Across the road, No. 18, built in 1877, was the home of Pre-Raphaelite artist William Holman Hunt, and here he completed his last and best-known work, *The Lady of Shalott*. He died in the house in 1910. Previously No. 18 was home to Cetshwayo, King of the Zulus during the Anglo-Zulu War of 1879, who stayed there during his visit to London to meet Queen Victoria and Prime Minister William Gladstone in 1882.

Standing in the fork between Melbury Road and Ilchester Place, and partly concealed by trees, is No. 31, Woodland

House, built in 1877 and designed by Norman Shaw in his trademark red brick for the artist Sir Luke Fildes, who lived there from the age of 32 until his death aged 83 in 1927. Edward VII sat for a state portrait in Fildes's large, centrally heated studio, lit by five huge windows on the north side of the house, and described it as '*one of the finest rooms in London*'. Woodland House then became the home of film producer Michael Winner, for over 40 years. It is currently owned by pop star Robbie Williams.

Tower House next door at No. 29 is also owned by a pop star, in this case Led Zeppelin guitarist Jimmy Page. This distinctive and slightly alarming thirteenth-century French Gothic house with its fairytale staircase tower and conical cap, was designed and built in 1878 by architect William Burges for himself. Burges seems to have based the design on his fantasy castle in South Wales, Castell Coch, which he was constructing at that time for the 3rd Marquess of Bute, and he was determined that his house should be different from the Queen Anne style that prevailed in the rest of the road and which he loathed. The interior of the Tower House was as High Victorian Gothic as the outside, the rooms dark with heavy wooden furniture, statues, deep velvet curtains, carvings over the fireplaces, murals, tapestries, friezes, painted ceilings, ceramic tiles, lots of marble and stained glass. The rooms all have different themes: Time, Love, the Liberal Arts, Animals, the Signs of the Zodiac. The entrance hall has a mosaic floor depicting a maze, at the centre of which Theseus is seen slaying the Minotaur. Burges's own bedroom was painted blue with illustrations of the sea and its inhabitants, so that he could imagine himself to be floating in the sea while in one of his opiate hazes. Burges, alas, had

No 8 Melbury Road

little time to enjoy his new home, the interior of which is still considered, even today, as one of the finest examples of medieval secular Gothic Revival, for he died there of a chill in 1881. Most of the furniture was sold off, but much of the extraordinary structural decoration remains.

No. 8, further along on the left, was built in 1877 for the artist Marcus Stone, illustrator of some of Charles Dickens's novels. Like Woodland House, this studio home was designed by Norman Shaw and incorporates his trademark red brick with tall, narrow white-painted sash windows. Stone's studio was on the first floor with light provided by the three oriel windows facing the road, the centre window being extended upwards for more light. Stone and Fildes became fiercely competitive over whose Norman Shaw designed studio home was better, with Fildes declaring that everyone agreed his house *'knocked Stone's to bits'*.

☞ CONTINUE STRAIGHT ON ALONG MELBURY ROAD AND GO PAST THE NO ENTRY SIGNS BESIDE THE BLOCK OF FLATS ON THE LEFT THAT WAS BUILT ON THE SITE OF G.F. WATTS'S STUDIO.

In contrast to the Queen Anne style of much of Melbury Road No. 13, on the right, was built in neo-classical form, in 1882. Next door, the Queen Anne style No. 9 was built as a single house by George Stephenson in 1880 and converted to two houses in 1935.

The block of properties opposite was built in 1876 for the sculptor Thomas Thornycroft, who created the statue of Queen Boudicca in her chariot that dominates the west end of Westminster Bridge, and his son Hamo Thornycroft, also a sculptor, whose statue of Oliver Cromwell stands outside the Houses of Parliament. This building, which consists of a pair of semi-detached houses divided by a huge chimney and a studio, was designed largely by Hamo Thornycroft himself, with help from architect Sir John Belcher. The Thornycrofts rented out one half of the semi-detached pair and lived in the other, while the studio was extended and divided up so that each member of the family had somewhere to work.

☞ NOW GO TO THE END OF MELBURY ROAD, TURN LEFT INTO ADDISON ROAD AND THEN LEFT INTO HOLLAND PARK ROAD.

③ Holland Park Road

The first red-brick house on the left, No. 32, was built in 1900 and designed by Albert Cockerell, as was No. 34 behind, which is accessed through an archway with above it a bust of an unidentified man. The row of two-storey red-brick cottages at Nos. 20–30 was built in 1879 as studio residences by Arthur Langdale and Company. The archway was kept democratically un-gated and each residence had large roof-lights facing north. The caricaturist and *Punch* cartoonist Philip May (1864–1903) lived at No. 20.

No. 14 next door was designed by the 'Father of Arts and Crafts Architecture', Philip Webb, who designed William Morris's Red House in Bexleyheath. It was built in 1866 for the artist Valentine Princep, whose father had lived in the original Little Holland House and been a friend of G.F. Watts. The design is artistically idiosyncratic, combining pointed gables and a flat parapet with a variety of windows, round, oriel and mock-Tudor.

(4)   **Lord Leighton's House**
(1865)

Frederic, Lord Leighton (1830–1896), was the grandson of the Russian royal family's senior physician and a wealthy man in his own right, but he was determined to become an artist on merit, an ambition he achieved in spectacular fashion in 1855 when Queen Victoria bought his first major painting. In 1878 he was made President of the Royal Academy and is still the only British artist to be elevated to the peerage. To cap it all he was buried in St Paul's Cathedral. Leighton House was begun in 1865, the first artist's studio home to be built in Holland Park in what would become a celebrated artist's colony. Designed very much to Leighton's specifications by his friend George Aitchison, the house began modestly as a small neo-Classical building in red

Suffolk brick with a north-facing studio overlooking the garden, but was extended and added to over the next 30 years to become a *'private palace of art'*.

To the west (left) of the main house a Turkish dome crowns the highlight of the house, the Arab Hall, added by Aitchison in 1877 and based on the twelfth-century Moslem palace of La Zisa in Palermo. The hall was built as somewhere to display Leighton's collection of Islamic tiles and is centred around a fountain and pool surrounded by Victorian mosaics. A gilded mosaic frieze by illustrator Walter Crane runs around the top of the room supported on capitals sculpted by Viennese-born sculptor J. Edgar Boehm (1834–1890), and there is work by Randolph Caldecott and other artists of the day. The brown-brick extension to the east houses extra gallery space, the Perrin Gallery, and was designed by Halsey Ricardo in 1927. Leighton House is now run as a museum and is the only studio home in Britain open to the public.

Next door, Nos. 10a and 10 are set back behind a large walled garden. They were built as one house in 1893 by E.E. and F. Brown as a studio home for the portrait painter Sir James Jebusa Shannon (1862–1923). No. 10, with the wide Dutch gable, incorporates the remains of the original farmhouse of the Holland House Estate. It later became the home of yet another *Punch* cartoonist, John Bernard Partridge.

Now go to the end of Holland Park Road and turn right into Melbury Road. Go to the end, cross Kensington High Street and turn left. Cross Earl's Court Road at the lights and turn right. At the Princess Victoria pub, first licensed in 1838 and rebuilt in its present form in 1860, turn left into Pater Street.

Warwick Chambers, the first of the two apartment blocks on the north side of Pater Street, was built in 1887 by a local surveyor, George Eves, and has the rather spartan look of social dwellings about it. The much more deluxe Abingdon Mansions next door were built in 1890 by George Eves's son William and were designed for the middle classes, hence 'Mansions' as opposed to 'Chambers'. At the end of the road the rather pretty Queen Anne style Kensington Arms was rebuilt as we see it in 1890 but is now, alas, no longer a pub. Turn left into Abingdon Road to see Ilchester Mansions on the left, built in 1892 by William Eves, and the fine Victorian shop fronts opposite, put up in 1881 by his father George.

☞ NOW TURN ROUND AND GO SOUTH ALONG ABINGDON ROAD OVER TWO MINI ROUNDABOUTS RIGHT TO THE END, WHERE YOU TURN LEFT INTO STRATFORD ROAD.

On the left, at No. 21a, a white-painted arch leads through to Scarsdale Studios, a set of small studio homes grouped around an internal courtyard built in 1891 for a community of artists. Note the elaborately carved name panel above the arch.

Carry on along Stratford Road, jinking right and left past the junction with Allen Street. On the left, just where the road begins to jink right again, are the Stratford Studios.

⑤ Stratford Studios
(1880)

A narrow passageway grandly called Stratford Avenue leads to ten studios built of red brick and sporting Dutch gables. They were built in 1880 and, like Scarsdale Studios, were put up by a local builder to take advantage of the artistic call that the area had exerted since the Great Exhibition in 1851.

Continue along Stratford Road to Marloes Road at the end. Note the drinking fountain across the road set into the wall of what was the Kensington workhouse in 1893 by Figgis T. Phillips. The inscription bids God *'to bless the poor and make them from strong drink free ...'* The workhouse became St Mary Abbot's Hospital, most of which was demolished in the 1990s, although you can still see the original brick gate posts a little further up the road. Turn right into Marloes Road, then next right into Lexham Gardens, which was laid out and built along in the 1870s and 80s. At the end turn left into Earl's Court Road, which dates from the same period. On the left-hand corner by the traffic lights at the junction with Cromwell Road is another Tower House, a white-brick Italianate villa with a distinctive belvedere tower with oval windows, built in 1872 by Thomas

Huggett. This was formerly the home of the London Academy of Music and Dramatic Art.

Cross Cromwell Road and continue along Earl's Court Road for about a third of a mile, past three Victorian pubs, all on the left: the Earls Court Tavern of 1866, the Prince of Teck, built by Thomas Huggett in 1868, and the Courtfield Hotel of 1876.

6 Collingham Gardens
(1880–8)

☞ TURN LEFT INTO BRAMHAM GARDENS AT THE FIRST TRAFFIC LIGHTS AFTER THE BLACKBIRD PUB, WHICH WAS CONVERTED FROM A BANK IN 1994. WALK TO THE END AND PREPARE FOR A TREAT.

We now enter the fantastical world of George and Peto. In front of you is Nos. 9–18 Collingham Gardens, a breathtaking array of gloriously outrageous houses of every conceivable design, all different, all magnificent, all way over the top, a riot of Flemish and Tudor, Renaissance, Gothic, Queen Anne, Dutch gables, square gables, stepped gables, red brick and terracotta, pink brick and terracotta, red brick and stone stripes, and more. These extraordinary hallucinations were built by Sir Ernest George and Harold Ainsworth Peto between 1880 and 1888 and were inspired by the Flemish and Bavarian houses they had come across and admired while travelling in Europe.

Turn right into Collingham Gardens. Go to the end and turn left into Bolton Gardens, where in 1866 Beatrix Potter was born, at No. 2, now gone and replaced by a school. Take the first left into Collingham Gardens, where on the left there

is another row of spectacular houses by George and Peto, in this case built between 1880 and 1886. Go to the roundabout and turn right into Harrington Gardens, lined on the right by more George and Peto, this time held together with first-floor arcades.

(7) William Gilbert's House
(1883)

The finest house of all is the Flemish No. 19, on the right, built in 1883 for the librettist Sir William Gilbert of Gilbert and Sullivan, and paid for out of the profits of their light operetta *Patience*. As noted by Beatrix Potter in her diary, the house is very handsome. Like Linley Sambourne's, Gilbert's house was decorated in the Aesthetic, or Artistic, style and filled with Oriental and other exotic objects, and was perhaps the last great hurrah of that style before the Arts and Crafts style came in. Gilbert wrote *The Mikado* in his study here, inspired, it is said, by the clattering fall of a Japanese sword that hung above the study door. Before you go, note the stone galleon that sits at the very top of the stepped gable, a reference to Gilbert's alleged ancestor the heroic Elizabethan sailor Sir Humphrey Gilbert.

☞ Now continue along Harrington Gardens as far as the roundabout, where you turn right into Ashburn Place, which leads to Wetherby Gardens.

Facing you are three houses with terracotta porticos. The one with the most exotic portico, No. 25, on the far right, was the home of the sculptor J. Edgar Boehm. He sculpted the columns of the portico himself and a few happy minutes may be spent looking for his signature amongst the sculptures.

☞ As you come from Ashburn Place turn left into Wetherby Gardens and follow along Wetherby Place and Hereford Square to Gloucester Road.

In front of you is the Hereford Arms, haunt of both J.M. Barrie and Sir Arthur Conan Doyle, who mentions the pub in *The Adventures of Sherlock Holmes*. A pub legend, which appears much more plausible after a pint or two, is that Conan Doyle named Sherlock Holmes after a nearby block of flats, although I have been unable as yet to find Sherlock Holmes Mansions.

☞ Turn left into Gloucester Road and second right into Stanhope Gardens. Walk along to Queen's Gate and turn right. St Augustine is across the road.

⑧ St Augustine, Queen's Gate
(1865)

The candy-striped red, yellow and white west front of St Augustine, with its large Gothic bell-cote, comes as a pleasant surprise amongst all the white stucco of Queen's Gate. The use of polychrome brick decoration marks it out as the work of William Butterfield, architect of the sublime All Saints, Margaret Street (*see* page 227).

The church sits at a jaunty angle to the street because the surrounding land was still being developed when construction began in 1865, although it wasn't completed until 1876. The interior is no less colourful than the outside, with more of Butterfield's polychrome brick and stone decoration, as well as marble, slates, mosaics and painted ceramic tiles on the walls.

☞ EXIT THE CHURCH AND TURN RIGHT (NORTH) ALONG QUEEN'S GATE. CROSS CROMWELL ROAD AND CONTINUE ON QUEEN'S GATE.

⑨ Queen's Gate
(c.1855)

Queen's Gate was laid out from 1855 onwards on land belonging to the Great Exhibition's Royal Commissioners. The west side is mainly identical terraced houses from the 1860s while the east side has a mix of modern Imperial College buildings and some fine individual Victorian terraced houses, particularly at the northern end. There are also a couple of interesting houses by Norman Shaw including No. 170, a simple New York style town house on the corner of Imperial College Road, which was built in 1889 and is a restrained, almost Georgian affair in Shaw's favourite red brick with white-painted windows and shutters. There are none of Shaw's usual elaborations and everything is in proportion. Very satisfying.

☞ CONTINUE ALONG QUEEN'S GATE AS FAR QUEEN'S GATE TERRACE. AT THIS POINT YOU MAY WISH TO CONTINUE A LITTLE FURTHER ON QUEEN'S GATE TO SEE NORMAN SHAW'S NO. 196, BUILT IN 1875 FOR J.P. HESELTINE, A WEALTHY STOCKBROKER, FRIEND OF WHISTLER AND TRUSTEE OF THE NATIONAL GALLERY. OTHERWISE TURN LEFT INTO QUEEN'S GATE TERRACE, WHICH IS IMPRESSIVELY LINED WITH TWO MAGNIFICENT TERRACES OF ITALIANATE WHITE STUCCO DATING FROM BETWEEN 1860 AND 1865.

At the far end of Queen's Gate Terrace, on the corner of Gloucester Road, you will be hard pressed not to notice a robust intrusion into the stucco by something a bit more individual, a pair of houses in Venetian Gothic built by Charles Gray in 1864. One of them is now occupied by Da Mario, pizza place to the stars.

Across the road is the Gloucester Arms, with a splendid late Victorian pub front of Corinthian columns.

☞ TURN RIGHT INTO GLOUCESTER ROAD.

On the right, where the road kinks left and right, is the helter-skelter tower of No. 1 Kensington Gate, the home in the 1860s of Richard Westmacott the Younger (1799–1872), sculptor of the pediment of the Royal Exchange in the City, who lived there with his family of six and five servants. The extraordinary round tower was described by writer and

Kensington resident Leigh Hunt, as *'one of those unmeaning rounded towers whose tops look like pepper boxes'*. Kensington Gate was built in 1847 on the site of the Kensington workhouse.

The road now becomes Palace Gate, which extends south from the main gate into the grounds of Kensington Palace, hence its name, and was created out of the northern section of Gloucester Road in 1865. No. 8, on the right, gives the impression of being all red brick, but when you look at it a little more closely it is in fact yellow brick with red-brick dressings and carved and moulded red brickwork. The house is separated from the street by iron railings, and there is a delightful wrought-iron balcony at first-floor level. The house was designed by the Scottish architect J.J. Stevenson in his favourite Queen Anne Revival style, and was one of the first houses in London to have fireproof floors and cavity walls. It was built in 1873 for a 31-year-old barrister with 'artistic inclinations' called Henry Francis Makins, who hailed from a family of Yorkshire bankers. Makins, whose fortune was derived from shrewd investments rather than triumphs at the Bar, was a keen collector of Pre-Raphaelite pictures, particularly the work of his near neighbour John Everett Millais. He gathered together a notable collection that has since been augmented by his descendants to form possibly the most important private collection of Pre-Raphaelite art in the world.

(10) No. 2 Palace Gate
(1878)

A little further along on the right, No. 2 is the famous 'big red house' of painter John Everett Millais. Along with William

Holman Hunt, Dante Gabriel Rossetti and four others, Millais was one of the founders of the Pre-Raphaelite Brotherhood, a secret society of rebellious young artists who wanted to choose their own direction rather than be dragooned into following the idealised style of painting of Raphael and the Renaissance masters, as favoured by Sir Joshua Reynolds and the Royal Academy. Millais's paintings proved hugely popular and he was soon earning up to £30,000 a year, the equivalent today of £2 million. In 1853 he was elected a full member of the Royal Academy. In 1885 he became the first artist ever to receive a hereditary title, when Queen Victoria personally created him a Baronet, of Palace Gate in the parish of St Mary Abbots, Kensington. On top of that she gave him special permission to fish in the Serpentine in Hyde Park.

Millais moved in to No. 2 with his family in 1878 and lived there for the rest of his life. The house, which was designed in a rather plain style by Philip Hardwick, was built to Millais's own specifications and was, according to the art critic Walter Armstrong, *'characteristic of the man – none of the thought out quaintness of the Anglo-Dutch revival but a great plain square house with an excrescence here and there where demanded by convenience'*. Another art critic, John Oldcastle, writing in the *Magazine for Art*, appreciated the fact that *'Mr Millais has built himself an artist's house into which the aestheticism of the day does not enter, no not by so much as a peacock fan.'* A dig, perhaps, at Frederic Leighton who, around the same time at the other end of Kensington High Street, was finishing off his rather more ostentatious artist's hovel that included an exotic 'Arab Hall' replete with strutting peacocks.

Unfortunately, Millais's studio, unlike those of some other Victorian artists, has not been preserved, but as you stand in front of the house today it is easy to hear the clip clop of horses and to imagine one of Millais's many distinguished visitors alighting from the carriage and disappearing in through the front door to have a portrait painted in the great man's cluttered atelier. Prime Ministers Gladstone, Disraeli and the Earl of Rosebery, the poet Lord Tennyson, the great actor-manager Henry Irving and the actress Lillie Langtry were just some of the prominent Victorians who sat for him. Another visitor was Millais's great friend the sugar baron and philanthropist Henry Tate, and it was over dinner at No. 2 in 1892 that Millais encouraged Tate to open a National Gallery of British Art, now known to us all as Tate Britain.

A number of the more luxurious fittings installed by Millais are said to have survived inside – carved marble fireplaces, Sicilian marble floors, the wrought-iron staircase balustrade and the marble basin of a much talked about fountain on the landing, into which water had once spouted from the mouth of a black marble seal, the work of J. Edgar Boehm.

Now occupied by the Zambian High Commission, No. 2 Palace Gate is certainly one of London's most sumptuous private houses and testament to the popularity of artists in the Victorian Age. As the writer Thomas Carlyle is purported to have asked when he visited No. 2, *'Has paint done all this, Mr Millais?' 'It has,'* replied Millais, happily. *'Then there are more fools in the world than I thought there were,'* said Carlyle.

In 1896, following the death of Lord Leighton, Millais was elected President of the Royal Academy, but died later that year of throat cancer and was buried in the crypt of St Paul's Cathedral.

☞ Continue up Palace Gate.

On the left, No. 1a, tall, thin and gabled with a Portland stone façade, is quite unlike any other house in the street. The original house on this site was built in 1862 for the author and friend of Charles Dickens's, John Forster (1812–1876), and it was while living here that Forster wrote his definitive *Life of Charles Dickens*, completed in 1874. In 1896 Forster's house was dramatically remodelled as we see it today by the Arts and Crafts architect C.J. Harold Cooper for William Alfred Johnstone, youngest son of the proprietor of the *Evening Standard*. The design is highly idiosyncratic, with a hint of Tudor and a whisper of Gothic, and caused quite a stir at the time. If you admire Harold Cooper's Arts and Crafts style you might find it worthwhile to seek out a similar house he designed the previous year, 1895, in Stratton Street, Mayfair. Green Park House, as it is called, previews many of the innovative features found here at No 1a.

☞ NOW GO TO THE END OF PALACE GATE, TURN LEFT
INTO KENSINGTON ROAD AND CONTINUE UNTIL YOU
REACH THE MILESTONE HOTEL ON THE LEFT, AT THE
ENTRANCE TO KENSINGTON COURT.

11 Kensington Court

Kensington Court stands on the site of Kensington House, a vast marble palace of 100 rooms built in 1873–5 by a flamboyant and unscrupulous Victorian financier called Baron Albert Grant MP (1831–1899), an early practitioner of what would one day be described as the '*unacceptable face of capitalism*'. He was the inspiration for the slippery Augustus Melmotte MP in Anthony Trollope's novel *The Way We Live Now* and was played unforgettably by David Suchet in the 2001 TV adaptation of the book. He is remembered, however, for one particularly noble gesture, made when he was still flush, which was to gift Leicester Square to the people of London.

Before he could move in to Kensington House, Baron Grant went bankrupt and the house – Grant's Folly or Swindle Towers, as it was affectionately known – was sold at auction in lots and taken down in 1882. The grand marble staircase was purchased by Madame Tussaud's and now graces their entrance hall in Marylebone Road, while the wrought-iron front gates now stand at the East Sheen entrance to Richmond Park, and another set of gates and railings can be found at Sandown Park racecourse.

In 1882 the freehold of the site was bought by property developer Jonathan T. Carr with the aim of building a new kind of elegant community for London's burgeoning middle classes. To make this a reality he hired the well-established architect J.J. Stevenson, a leader in the popular Queen Anne style and the man behind No. 8 Palace Gate.

Stevenson began with the most prestigious plot, now No. 1 Kensington Court, which fronts on to Kensington Road. It is a large, ornate building of pink brick and terracotta with Dutch gables, flamboyantly carved hoods over the windows, a wrought-iron balcony at first-floor level and a big, squat, red and white stone porch sheltering the front door steps. To the left of this is an archway, which led through to a stable yard but is now bricked up. No. 1 was built for a Mrs Anne Marie Lucena and is now the Milestone Hotel, which takes its name from an old milestone set in the railings at the front. This marks the turnpike that stood here on the road out of London, which is indicated by a pointing finger as being 1½ miles (2.4 km) to the east.

No. 2 has its main entrance round the corner in Kensington Court itself, but shows its most exuberant side to Kensington Road. It was built in 1883 for 25-year-old Athelstan Riley, a grandson of the founder of the Union Bank (now part of the Royal Bank of Scotland, via NatWest). Riley, who could perhaps be described as a man who had little need to toil at the coal face, wanted an exceptional house for this prominent site, one that would be distinct from No. 1 and that would stand out from the Queen Anne terraces that J.J. Stevenson had planned for the rest of Kensington Court. At the time Riley was a graduate at Oxford and so he chose for the project T.G. Jackson, an eminent architect known for his work on many of the Oxford colleges, including the Bridge of Sighs connecting two parts of Hertford College. Jackson, whose only London town house this would sadly prove to be, certainly created something eye-catching and different for No. 2. Oxford comes to Kensington in a striking mix of Flemish Gothic and early Tudor brick and terracotta. In the way that Henry VIII had the initials 'H' and 'A' (for Henry and Anne Boleyn) carved into the stonework of his palaces, so did Athelstan Riley have his initials carved all over No. 2, on the string courses and above the first-floor windows. Look out also for the delicious ground-floor library bay window near the corner, with a lead cap of writhing sea dragons inspired by the spire of the Copenhagen Exchange, the two small, square windows of the chapel to the right of the recessed front door, also decorated with swirling sea monsters, and the dancing 'putti' below the windows of the second floor facing Kensington Road.

At the time No. 2 was variously described as attracting the *'admiring cynosure of the many wayfarers who pass along this thronging route of London traffic'* and, by a rather more pompous expert, as a *'design of dubious origin and wanton ornament'*.

☞ NOW TURN LEFT INTO KENSINGTON COURT AND FOLLOW TO THE END, RIGHT AND LEFT.

No. 3 is the first in a long, L-shaped terrace of red-brick Queen Anne houses, each with balconies on the first floor contained by wrought-iron railings and carried on shallow arches, the whole row connected by an elaborate frieze above the first-floor windows. J.J. Stevenson was responsible for designing this earliest section of Kensington Court, which was built between 1883 and 1886. It stretches all the way around the dog leg from No. 3 to No. 25 at the southern extremity, and includes a smaller island block to the west, so the impression here is of a harmonious whole with just slight variations to each individual house. What could be rather gloomy, menacing canyons of dark red brick are rendered bright and cheery by lashings of white paint, flowery embellishments and patterns in terracotta and stone, lots of decorative ironwork, window boxes on the balconies and beside the doors, and some tall plane trees.

At the southern end of the development is Kensington Court Mews, built in 1886 as somewhere for the first residents to stable their horses and carriages. On the ground floor are garages for the coaches, while the horses were stabled on the first floor, which was reached by ramps. Above the stables were rooms for the grooms and other servants. The stables and the servants' quarters have been neatly converted into rather nice apartments, accessed by individual stairways, while the garages below now house carriages of a horseless variety.

Further on, squeezed into a recess between the Mews and the vast mansion block of Kensington Court Gardens, is a plain, unassuming five-storey yellow brick building quite out of kilter with the opulence of the rest of Kensington Court. A discreet brass plaque by the comically grand front door informs us that this is …

⑫ The Old Pump House

Here is evidence of one of the many ingenious innovations that make Kensington Court so interesting, in this case hydraulics. Hydraulics was the latest thing in the 1880s, a clean, quiet and reliable alternative to steam, and Jonathan T. Carr, the original developer, wanted all the houses to have hydraulically operated service lifts instead of back stairs. To this end he prevailed upon the newly formed London Hydraulic Power Company to build a pumping station just for Kensington Court, unconnected to the company's main supply. Water drawn from the Thames was pumped from the Old Pump House here to the other houses through pipes running along subways dug under the road. This was the very first time an independent hydraulic system had been used to power domestic houses anywhere in Britain, possibly in the world, and it was quite rightly considered a marvel. The Old Pump House didn't have windows originally but was simply a brick tower housing a giant accumulator, boilers and pumping engines.

Unfortunately, it soon proved uneconomic for Kensington Court to have its own bespoke system. In 1892 the pump house was shut and the estate was connected up to the main hydraulic supply. Some of the lifts continued to use hydraulic power for another 35 years or so, but gradually Kensington Court was weaned off hydraulics and on to electricity. The Pump House was converted into a rather nice residence.

Now walk back towards Kensington High Street along the west side of Kensington Court. Where the road widens into a short stretch of cobbles turn and look up at the modest stone plaque above the doorway of the Warner Chappell offices. Chiselled on to it are the words, 'Electrical Lighting Station'.

13   Electrical Lighting Station

Housed in this building was one of the very first public electrical lighting stations in the world, and the lucky

denizens of Kensington Court were residents of the first housing development in the world to be supplied with their own electricity on a permanent basis.

The site of the lighting station had originally been set aside for stables, but the architect J.J. Stevenson had from the very start anticipated the introduction of electrical lighting for Kensington Court, and the subways that had been dug beneath the road for the hydraulics system were always intended for electrical use as well.

Stevenson knew who to turn to – his nephew was an electrical engineer and was then working in Vienna with the foremost electrical practitioner of the day, Colonel Rookes Crompton, who was busy installing electrical lighting in Vienna's theatres. Crompton was shown around Kensington Court in 1885 and in late 1886 he erected a temporary wooden generating station on the north-west corner of the estate with, inside it, a Willans steam engine coupled to a dynamo and a boiler adapted from a locomotive. The station became operative in early 1887 and transmitted direct current electricity along copper wires resting on porcelain insulators fixed to brackets on the walls of the subways. Every house had a battery that was charged each day at dusk, and extra power could be supplied direct from the generating station if required.

As demand grew, so came the need for a bigger and more reliable system, and in 1889 the wooden structure was replaced with the brick building we see today. Inside, set in a large basement turbine hall, were three boilers feeding seven powerful Willan-Crompton steam generators. Such was the success of this new Kensington station that Crompton went on to build similar stations all over the world.

Throughout the 1890s Kensington and Knightsbridge continued to expand rapidly and demand for electricity soared. By 1900 the Kensington Court station had become too small to supply the ever-increasing demand and was converted into a sub-station linked to Crompton's main power station at Shepherd's Bush. The building was finally decommissioned and stripped out in 1985 and is now offices.

Back in Kensington Court Passage there is a blue plaque on the wall showing that *'Colonel R.E.B. Crompton 1845–1940 Electrical Engineer lived and worked here 1891–1939'*.

Yorkshireman Colonel Rookes Evelyn Bell Crompton was inspired to become an engineer and inventor after a visit to the Great Exhibition when he was aged six. He was an early pioneer of electric lighting and the electrical industry and his company Crompton & Co. was the world's first large-scale manufacturer of electrical equipment. He worked closely on domestic lighting with Joseph Swan, inventor of the light bulb, and was responsible for installing the first electrical lighting systems at Windsor Castle, Holyrood Palace in Edinburgh, the Law Courts in the Strand, Kings Cross station and the Vienna Opera House. Under a number of different guises the company continued to flourish until 1968, when it was taken over by the Hawker Siddeley aerospace group. Since then the various bits of the company have gone their separate ways but Crompton Lamps, the oldest lamp maker in the world, now trades independently again, from premises in Bradford.

Once the power station at Kensington Court was up and running Colonel Crompton had a house built next to it in the same Tudor style, No. 48 Kensington Court or 'Thriplands'. As well as being an electrical engineer, Crompton was also a keen structural engineer and his new house was to be no less radical and ground-breaking than his power station. In Crompton's own words, *'My house was I believe one of the earliest to be built in England on the modern principle of framed steel girders on which the outer and inner brickwork is supported.'*

Since the house was built in 1889, No. 48 Kensington Court has a claim to being the first steel-framed building in Britain.

The top two floors of No. 48 were kitted out as a laboratory, making good use of the ready power supply from next door. In this lab Crompton developed the world's first electric toaster, the

Eclipse, based on an idea by a Scotsman, Alan MacMasters, and also the world's first practical electric oven, both of which were manufactured by Crompton & Co.

(14) Palace Green
(c.1862–3)

Now return to Kensington High Street, turn left and cross the road at the pedestrian lights. Turn right and then immediately left into Palace Green, a short stretch of private road laid out in the 1850s on the site of the kitchen gardens of Kensington Palace.

Immediately on the left is No. 1, a tall, unusual red-brick house built in 1863 for the 9th Earl of Carlisle by Philip Webb. The Earl was a friend and patron to the Pre-Raphaelite Brotherhood and an artist in his own right, which explains the strange recessed arch in the north face of the house. It once contained a staircase running from the Earl's studio on the first floor directly into the garden. The windows are a very early example of the Queen Anne style windows subsequently made popular by Norman Shaw. The interior had originally been lavishly furnished and decorated by William Morris, but that work has gone and the building is now apartments.

Next door we come to one of the most interesting houses of Victorian London, No. 2 Palace Green, currently serving as the Israeli embassy. This was the last home of the writer William Makepeace Thackeray, regarded by the Victorians as second only to, if not equal to, Charles Dickens as an author, but today known mainly for the novel *Vanity Fair*. Originally the home of the Royal Ranger, No. 2 was in a badly dilapidated state when

Thackeray bought it in 1860 and he virtually had to rebuild the entire house. He oversaw the design of the rebuild himself and the result was one of the very first Queen Anne Revival houses, or neo-Georgian houses, some time before neo-Georgian became the latest thing. Thackeray's house in Palace Green thus marked a new beginning in Victorian architecture away from the Gothic so popular up until then. Equally innovative was Thackeray's choice of red brick – he declared proudly that his new house would be *'the reddest house in all the town'* and the artist John Millais, who lived nearby, commented that Thackeray had *'first set the fashion for red brick'*.

Thackeray moved into No. 2 Palace Green in March 1862 but was granted just a short time to enjoy his new home. He died there in his sleep, of a stroke, after returning from a dinner party on Christmas Eve 1863. He was aged just 52. His body was taken from here to be buried in Kensal Green cemetery in front of two thousand mourners.

☞ RETURN TO KENSINGTON HIGH STREET AND TURN RIGHT. ON THE CORNER OF KENSINGTON CHURCH STREET, AT THE VERY POINT WHERE KENSINGTON BEGAN, STANDS ST MARY ABBOTS CHURCH.

(15) # St Mary Abbots
(1869–72)

The original Norman church on the site now occupied by St Mary Abbots was rebuilt several times before the present building was erected in 1869–72. It is a classic, if unexceptional example of a large Victorian church, a mixture of Early English style and neo-Gothic, and was designed by Sir George Gilbert

Vestry Hall

Scott, the architect of the moment, who was then working just up the road on the Albert Memorial. The spire of St Mary Abbots, which imitates that of St Mary Redcliffe in Bristol, rises elegantly from a cluster of fine pinnacles to a height of 278 feet (85 m), and is the tallest spire in London. A delightful feature is the Gothic arcaded cloister leading from the little square to the church door, which was added by John Oldrid Scott, son of Sir George, in 1889.

☞ Now continue along Kensington High Street for High Street Kensington Station and the end of the walk.

On your way you will see on the right Kensington's first Town Hall, the quaint pink-brick and stone neo-Tudor Vestry Hall of 1852. It later became the home of Kensington's first public library and today is occupied by a bank.

End of walks: High Street Kensington Station

Recommended Places for Refreshment

The Princess Victoria 25 Earl's Court Road, W8

The Earls Court Tavern 123 Earl's Court Road, SW5

The Prince of Teck 161 Earl's Court Road, SW5

The Courtfield 167 Earl's Court Road, SW5

The Hereford Arms 127 Gloucester Road, SW7

The Queen's Arms 30 Queen's Gate Mews, SW7

The Gloucester Arms 34 Gloucester Road, SW7

The Goat 3a Kensington High Street, W8

The Greyhound 1 Kensington Square, W8

The Prince of Wales 8 Kensington Church Street, W8

THE CITY

—

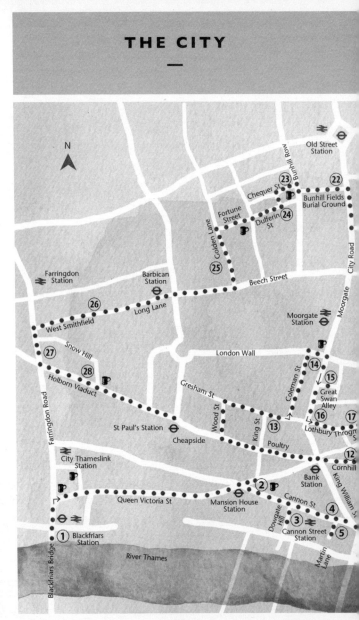

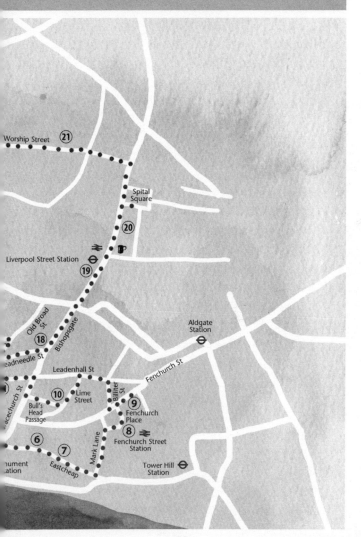

Chapter 3
Walking in the Victorian City

On this part of the walks we explore the historic centre of London. During the Victorian Age, London was the world's financial and commercial centre and the buildings that survived the bombing of the Second World War reflect this, with banks, livery companies, warehouses and offices dominating and few domestic dwellings. Amongst the modern skyscrapers and office blocks, however, there are some wonderful examples of Victorian architecture. We also step out of the City to see some rather special artisan's dwellings and the best Victorian lavatories in London.

Numbers applied to each attraction refer to the numbers on the map

Walks

Start walking: Blackfriars Station

The name Blackfriars comes from the black–robed monks of a Dominican monastery that stood on the site from 1278 to 1538. Blackfriars underground station opened in 1870 as the new eastern terminus of the Metropolitan District Railway, but has been heavily redeveloped and there is little left of the original structure, certainly above the surface, that is recognisable.

① **Blackfriars Bridges**
(1864, 1869, 1886)

☞ EXIT THE STATION AND TURN LEFT FOR BLACKFRIARS BRIDGE.

The simple red–brick and stone building on your left was built in 1873 as a Victorian office block. The name, Bridge House, is written under a parapet on the roof. The rather fine drinking fountain in front of the building was erected in 1861 by Samuel Gurney, Chairman of the Metropolitan Free Drinking Fountain Association. Now walk a little way on to the bridge. Standing in the river on the left are the abandoned piers of the first railway bridge to cross the Thames here. It was built by Joseph Cubitt in 1862–4 to carry the London, Chatham and Dover Railway (LCDR) across the river to stations in the City. This bridge was dismantled in 1985, leaving just the piers. Joseph Cubitt also built the current road bridge running parallel to his railway bridge and this was opened by Queen Victoria in 1869 – note the pier heads shaped like pulpits in honour of the Black Friars. The present railway bridge further to the east was built in 1884–6 by Sir John Wolfe-Barry and Henry Marc Brunel, son of Isambard Kingdom Brunel, to bring LCDR trains into a station opened in 1886. This was to provide an interchange with the underground station. Both the station and the bridge were then called St Paul's, the name being changed to Blackfriars in 1937 to avoid confusion with the new St Paul's Station on the Central Line. Engraved on the façade of the St Paul's railway station here at Blackfriars were the names of 54 cities in Britain and Europe that were served from St Paul's, such as Berlin, Paris, Florence, Geneva and even St Petersburg. The engraved destinations were saved during the rebuilding of the station and have been arranged as a wall in the new main concourse.

☞ RETURN TO THE STATION TO SEE THE DESTINATION WALL AND THEN LEAVE THE STATION AND TURN RIGHT INTO QUEEN VICTORIA STREET, LAID OUT IN 1867–71 ABOVE THE NEW DISTRICT RAILWAY EXTENSION TO MANSION HOUSE.

Immediately across the road is the Black Friar pub, London's very own 'flatiron' building, built in 1875 and redeveloped in Art Nouveau style in the early 1900s. Inside is breathtaking – a riot of marble and mosaics, carvings and mottoes and, upon the walls, numerous bronze statues of friars engaged in their duties. Well worth a visit at any time, the Black Friar is one of London's most interesting and unusual pubs.

☞ CONTINUE UNDER THE RAILWAY BRIDGE ALONG QUEEN VICTORIA STREET, WHICH IS TODAY LINED MOSTLY WITH MODERN BLOCKS.

Not far along, on the corner of St Andrew's Hill to the left, the small red-brick building that looks like a New York fire station used to be the Baynards Castle pub, first registered as such in 1878.

A short walk up St Andrew's Hill is the Cockpit pub, which stands on or near the site of William Shakespeare's home in Ireland Yard and was established in the eighteenth century as a venue for cockfighting. The sport was banned by the Victorians in 1849 and the pub was redeveloped around 1860 while retaining the spectator's gallery.

Back in Queen Victoria Street, past the Church of St Andrew by the Wardrobe, is No. 146, an Italianate palazzo designed in 1867 by the City architect Edward l'Anson and possibly his best work. Formerly the headquarters of the Bible Society, it is now home to the Church of Scientology.

☞ NOW WALK FOR 5 MINUTES PAST A NUMBER OF CHARACTERLESS MODERN OFFICE BLOCKS UNTIL THE ROAD BEGINS TO CURVE TO THE LEFT.

(2) **Albert Buildings**
(1869)

In the distance dwarfed by the modern blocks around it, you will see a rare Victorian survivor occupying the triangle formed by Queen Victoria Street, Cannon Street and Queen Street. This is Albert Buildings, a Gothic gem designed by Frederick J. Ward in 1869. The long façade on Queen Victoria Street, elegantly folded round at each end, is glorious to behold, three storeys of marching rows of windows, with different arches on each storey, divided by heavy decorated cornices.

Having admired Albert Buildings from Queen Victoria Street retrace your steps and, keeping Albert Buildings on your left, turn into Cannon Street. On your left is the Sugar Loaf pub, first recorded as such in 1839 and named for the many small sugar refineries once located south of Cannon Street.

③ Cannon Street Station
(1866)

Carry on along Cannon Street and turn right on to Dowgate Hill by the entrance to Cannon Street Station. On the right at Nos. 11–13 is the Dyers' Hall, which was opened in 1842 and designed, appropriately enough, by Charles Dyer, his only major work in London. From the end of Dowgate Hill you can get a good view of the surviving yellow-brick walls of the original Station, which was built in 1866 by Sir John Hawkshaw, with a hotel by Edward Barry at the front. The walls supported a huge semicircular, single-span arch made of glass and iron, 700 feet (213 m) long and 106 feet (32 m) high and ended in twin Wren-style towers facing the river, the eastern one of which contained a water tank that was used to power the station's hydraulics and replenish the steam engines. The station was badly bombed in the Second World War and the arch was removed in 1958, but the twin towers still stand – you can see the western tower from here – and most of the brickwork of the walls is original.

Now return to Cannon Street. Across the road, opposite the main station entrance, No. 103 is a splendid Veneto-Byzantine affair built in 1866, the same year as the station, by Fred Jameson for the Registered Land Company. Note how perfectly the window lights halve in width but double in number as the building rises.

④ St Mary Abchurch House, Cannon Street
(1895)

☞ CONTINUE EAST ALONG CANNON STREET WITH THE STATION ON YOUR RIGHT.

St Mary Abchurch House, on the left at Nos. 123–127, all red brick and terracotta with one pointed gable and one square, was designed by Herbert Huntly-Gordon and built in 1895. Huntly-Gordon worked closely with Doulton and Co. of Lambeth to produce the decorative terracotta used here, and there is a lively frieze above the third-floor windows showing naked cherubs engaged in all sorts of activities, unloading cargo from sailing ships, construction work, planning meetings, playing musical instruments – alas, the frieze is too high up to ascertain exactly what it is that they are doing but they are undoubtedly hard at work.

St Martin's Rectory
(1851)

A bit further along, step into Martin Lane on your right for an unexpected treat, a little taste of Italy. Here, rising incongruously from the midst of bland modern office architecture is a delightful Italianate campanile that could have been transported direct from Tuscany. It belongs, in fact, to St Martin's Rectory, built in 1851 on the site of St Martin Ongar church, which was demolished in 1820. The architect was John Davies, District Surveyor to Tower Hamlets, who was clearly influenced by his extensive travels in Italy in the 1820s. The large clock attached to the tower at first-floor level is dated 1853.

☞ RETURN TO CANNON STREET AND CONTINUE EASTWARDS ALONG THE SOUTH SIDE TO THE RATHER COMPLICATED KING WILLIAM STREET JUNCTION AHEAD. CROSS KING WILLIAM STREET AT THE LIGHTS AND GO STRAIGHT AHEAD INTO EASTCHEAP.

No. 23 Eastcheap
1861

☞ CROSS OVER EASTCHEAP WHEN YOU CAN AND WALK ALONG AS FAR AS PHILPOT LANE WHERE A ROW OF RATHER FINE VICTORIAN WAREHOUSES BEGINS.

First off, occupying the north-west corner plot, No. 23 is a marvellous example of colourful Lombardic Gothic, with barley twist window columns on the first floor, decorated cornices, polychromatic brick and stonework and carvings of animal heads in the eaves. It was built in 1861 by John Young & Sons as offices and warehousing for a firm of spice merchants called Messrs Hunt & Crombie and more than holds its own against the looming bulk of the Walkie Talkie behind. On the side of the building facing Philpot Lane, where the ground-floor cornice breaks, you can find London's smallest public sculpture, two tiny mice gnawing at a piece of cheese, put there, allegedly, to commemorate two workmen who accused each other of eating the other's sandwich and, while squabbling over the matter, fell off the scaffolding to their deaths.

Nos. 33–35 Eastcheap
(1868)

A couple of doors further along Eastcheap is one of London's most eccentric displays of Victorian whimsy, a tumult of red brick, stone carvings, sharp Gothic arches and heavy Gothic canopies and gables. Built in 1868 as offices and warehousing for a firm of Worcestershire vinegar makers called Hill & Evans, Nos. 33–35 was designed by Robert Lewis Roumieu, architect

of the Islington Literary and Scientific Society, now the Almeida Theatre. Poking out of the foliage carved on a medallion above the windows in the central Gothic arch on the second floor is the head of a wild boar, celebrating the famous Boars Head Tavern that stood nearby and was where Prince Hal and Sir John Falstaff caroused in Shakespeare's *Henry IV* plays.

Continue along Eastcheap to where a tree obscures the gorgeous early Victorian shop front of No. 43, which stands at right angles to the entrance of St Margaret Pattens church. The huge square bay window is flanked by matching doors with Corinthian columns.

Walk on towards the copper spire of All Hallows by the Tower and turn left opposite the Hung Drawn and Quartered pub into Mark Lane. Nos. 59–61, simple Venetian Gothic, was built in 1864 as offices for the Innes Brothers' City of London Real Property Company by George Aitchison, who would go on to design Lord Leighton's House in Kensington (*see* page 56). Behind the stone façade the building is constructed largely around an iron framework and boasts an elaborate iron staircase.

8 Fenchurch Street Station
(1854)

Continue along Mark Lane and turn right into London Street for Fenchurch Street Station. The original station was built in 1841 by Sir William Tite, architect of the Royal Exchange, for the London and Blackwall Railway and was the first railway terminus in the City. Until 1849 steam locomotives were not used and the carriages were hauled back and forth by steam-driven cables powered by stationary boilers at Fenchurch Street and Blackwall. As they approached Fenchurch Street Station the carriages were detached from the cables and completed their journey into the station under their own momentum. When it was time for the carriages to leave the station they were given a gentle push by the platform staff and gravity did the rest. The present station façade was built in 1854 and designed by George Berkeley.

9 Lloyds Register of Shipping
(1899)

Go past the station along Fenchurch Place, turn right into Fenchurch Street and walk past the Georgian East India Arms to the headquarters of the Lloyds Register of Shipping at No. 71, an impressive Arts and Crafts Baroque affair built in 1899–1900 and designed by Thomas Collcutt, architect of the Savoy Hotel. The sculptures above the ground-floor windows and doors are by George Frampton, a leading light of the New Sculpture movement whose members aimed for a more naturalistic, lifelike style of sculpture.

Retrace your steps west along Fenchurch Street past the East India Arms, cross at the pedestrian lights then left and right into Billiter Street. Take a good look at Nos. 19–21, dated 1865, architect unknown, as this is the only building in the street that will not shortly be demolished for the development of a new office block at No. 40 Leadenhall Street. Instead it will be restored and integrated into the scheme.

Leadenhall Market
(1881)

Continue along Billiter Street and turn left into Leadenhall Street. Take the first left into Lime Street, walk past the new Lloyds Building and turn right. Ahead is Leadenhall Market, tucked away amongst a warren of streets and alleyways on the site of the Roman basilica at what was the heart of the old Roman city. The market is one of London's oldest, dating from the early 1300s, and originally sold mostly meat, poultry and other foodstuffs. It was covered over and laid out in its present form by City architect Sir Horace Jones in 1881. Three stretches of cobbled lane, covered by roofs of wrought iron and glass meet beneath an iron and glass dome supported by wrought-iron columns. The Victorian colour scheme of maroon red and cream, with dark green for the shop window frames, has been superbly recreated and the whole effect is most attractive. Today the market shops sell every kind of item from clothes to greetings cards, but many of them still have wrought-iron hooks outside on which produce was once hung, a remnant from the days of meat and poultry.

Leadenhall Market was used as a location for the very first Harry Potter film, *Harry Potter and the Philosopher's Stone* (2001). To see the entrance to the Leaky Cauldron and Diagon Alley, walk south from the central dome, between two wrought-iron columns bearing no entry traffic signs As the lane curves left, turn right into Bull's Head Passage and the entrance is on your right at No. 42..

> ☞ CONTINUE ALONG BULL'S HEAD PASSAGE AND TURN RIGHT INTO GRACECHURCH STREET. A LITTLE FURTHER ALONG ON THE RIGHT IS THE BRICK, GABLED MAIN ENTRANCE TO LEADENHALL MARKET. AT THE TRAFFIC LIGHTS TURN LEFT INTO CORNHILL.

(11) Cornhill

On the right, the narrow, three-bay building with decorated terracotta strings (No. 65), just beyond the entrance to White Lion Court, is by Edward l'Anson. The Italianate building next to it, Nos. 66–67, was built in 1880 for the London and Lancashire Life Assurance Company by Thomas Chatfield Clarke. Opposite, No. 55, somewhat incongruous in red terracotta, was built in 1893 and designed by Ernest Runtz, better known for designing theatres. This building too, with its turret and gable, certainly has a whisper of the theatrical about it.

A little further along on the left, set back from the street, is the Italian Gothic porch of St Michael Cornhill, added to Christopher Wren's church by Sir George Gilbert Scott in 1860. The high relief sculpture of *St Michael Disputing with Satan* on the tympanum is by John Birnie Philip, who worked a lot with Scott and later sculpted the *Frieze of Parnassus* on Scott's Albert Memorial. Scott also re-ordered the interior of the church, which Wren had rebuilt after the Great Fire, in grand Victorian style and here we have one of the most interesting Victorian interiors in the City, well worth a look.

Further down on the left, on the corner of Birchin Lane, No. 42 is by Benjamin Tabberer and was built in 1877. The fine mahogany doors of No. 32, also on the left, are decorated with relief carvings of local historical events. One of the panels shows William Makepeace Thackeray meeting Anne and Charlotte Brontë, for this was formerly the office of their publisher Smith, Elder & Co, who occupied what was then No. 65. In 1848 Anne and Charlotte travelled here from Yorkshire to meet with their publisher and prove to him that they actually were Acton and Currer Bell. Their arrival caused something of a stir, for the publisher had thought the Bells were men. Nonetheless, once he had recovered from his surprise, he arranged for them to meet here with Charlotte's hero Thackeray for what turned out to be a rather strained occasion. In 1859 the *Cornhill Magazine* was published here for the first time, with Thackeray as the editor.

Retrace your steps to the lights and cross the road into the pedestrianised Royal Exchange Buildings to see the statues of two prominent 'foreign' Victorians, the German-born Paul Julius Reuter, who founded the worldwide news agency, and the American philanthropist George Peabody, who established the Peabody Trust. Reuter's head is seen atop a granite column and was crafted by Michael Black in 1976. Peabody's statue, in which he is shown seated, was erected here in 1869, the year of his death, and is the work of the American sculptor William Wetmore Story.

Walk back to Cornhill and turn right. The plinth in the middle of the road hides a ventilation shaft for the underground railway, which is most appropriate since the statue on top is of the Victorian civil engineer James Henry Greathead (1844–1896), renowned for his work on the London Underground. Greathead invented a tunnelling shield which was used in the construction of the Tower Subway in 1869, only the second tunnel to be dug under the River Thames. He was also responsible for extending the Metropolitan Railway to Hammersmith and the District Railway to Richmond and was engineer for the world's first electric deep-level tube line, the City and South London Railway, now part of the Northern Line. The statue was unveiled in 1994.

Royal Exchange
(1844)

At the Greathead statue go right for the Royal Exchange, founded on this site by Sir Thomas Gresham in 1566. This is the third Royal Exchange building here and was designed in typically early Victorian impure Classical style by Sir William Tite between 1841 and 1844. The 17 figures in the vast pediment have Commerce at their centre and were sculpted by Richard Westmacott (1775–1856). Inside, the courtyard was originally open but was glazed over in

1880. Painted on the walls, and missed by most visitors because they are obscured by the shops that now occupy the Exchange, are some of London's finest murals, depicting historic scenes. A balcony runs around the walls behind the shops and restaurants from which you can see the murals. Look out for lost Victorian masterpieces such as *Phoenicians trading with Early Britons* by Lord Leighton (1895), *William the Conqueror granting a charter to the Citizens of London* by John Seymour Lucas (1898), *Richard III being offered the Crown at Baynard's Castle* by Sigismund Goetze (1898), *The Opening of the first Royal Exchange by Elizabeth I* by Ernest Crofts (1899), *Charles I demanding the Five Members at the Guildhall* by Solomon J. Solomon (1897), *The Great Fire of London* by Stanhope Forbes (1899) and *The Opening of the third Royal Exchange by Queen Victoria in 1844* by Robert Macbeth (1895).

Leave the Royal Exchange by the main entrance. Ahead of you steps lead down to some of the world's earliest public lavatories, opened here in 1855. The equestrian statue is of the Duke of Wellington and was crafted out of bronze from captured French guns by Francis Chantrey who died before it could be finished, in 1841. The work was completed by Henry Weekes and unveiled in 1844. The Duke of Wellington is the only person to be the subject of two bronze equestrian statues in London.

☞ NOW CROSS CORNHILL TO YOUR LEFT, THEN LOMBARD STREET, TURN RIGHT AND WALK IN FRONT OF THE MANSION HOUSE AND BEAR LEFT.

The palazzo style building in front of you in Queen Victoria Street, which now serves as the City of London Magistrates

Court, was built for the National Safe Deposit in 1873 by John Whichcord Jr.

☞ NOW CROSS QUEEN VICTORIA STREET AND BEAR LEFT INTO POULTRY, WHICH SOON BECOMES CHEAPSIDE. CROSS OVER WHEN YOU CAN AND WALK ALONG CHEAPSIDE FOR ABOUT 500 YARDS (470 M) UNTIL YOU COME TO A LARGE PLANE TREE ON THE CORNER OF WOOD STREET THAT MARKS THE SITE OF ST PETER CHEAP CHURCH.

Crouched beneath the protective branches is a rare and extremely pretty small Victorian shop, at one time delightfully called 'Under the Tree'.

(13) No. 20 King Street, formerly 42 Gresham Street
(1850)

Turn right into Wood Street, walk to the top and turn right into Gresham Street, which was created in 1845 by widening a number of the surrounding lanes. Just after St Lawrence Jewry church, on the corner of King Street is what used to be 42 Gresham Street and is now labelled 20 King Street. Built in 1850 and designed by Sancton Wood, a cousin of Robert Smirke, architect of the main block of the British Museum, 20 King Street is considered to be one of London's more innovative mid-Victorian commercial buildings. Over the ground floor windows we see the earliest examples of a particular type of arch which was to become very popular in Victorian architecture. The arch has an arc of less than 180 degrees and is known as a 'segmental' arch. The bottom elements on each side of the arch, those which rest upon the Tuscan columns that keep the arch up, are known as 'springers'. In this case the springers are vertical, and this configuration of segmental arches on vertical springers was, at the time, both new and distinctive.

Armourers' Hall
(1840)

Continue along Gresham Street and take the second left into Coleman Street. No. 81, on the right-hand side at the end where the street meets London Wall, is the Armourers' Hall, used by the Armourers and Brasiers' Company, standing on a site that the Armourers have occupied since 1346. The present hall is the third on the site and was designed by J.H. Good in 1840 – you can tell by the Georgian feel that this is a very early Victorian building.

Institute of Chartered Accountants
(1890)

Now turn right into London Wall. On your left is The Globe, established as a pub in the late 1830s and remodelled in the 1870s. Turn right into Moorgate. On your right Nos. 63–73, with its plain Palladian façade, is from the 1840s, probably by Sir Robert Smirke. Cross Moorgate when you can and turn left into Great Swan Alley for the glorious Institute of Chartered Accountants headquarters, one of the first neo-Baroque buildings in London and great masterpiece of the Baroque specialist John Belcher. It was built in 1890. Much of the exterior sculpture work is by Belcher's great friend Hamo Thornycroft, famous for the statue of Oliver Cromwell outside the Palace of Westminster, and leading figure in the New Sculpture movement, along with George Frampton (Lloyds Register of Shipping).

Return to Moorgate and turn left (south). Across the road Nos. 13–15, with the elaborate polygonal turret and spire, was built in 1890 and designed by Aston Webb, architect of the Victoria and Albert Museum.

No. 7 Lothbury
(1866)

At the end of Moorgate turn left into Lothbury, with the blank wall of the Bank of England on your right. On the left, just past St Margaret Lothbury church, the Venetian Gothic No. 7 is one of the City's most imaginative surviving Victorian office blocks. Designed by George Somers Clarke, who worked with Sir Charles Barry on the Palace of Westminster, it was built in 1866 as the new head office for the General Credit and Discount Company. Decorative features include twisted shafts and black marble columns, while separating the second-floor windows on the Lothbury side is a stone frieze of eight figures representing trade and commerce. The arched doorway on to Lothbury was originally located around the side of the building on Tokenhouse Yard and was moved to the front in 1900. Note the address carved in sandstone by the door.

No 7 Lothbury

 Throgmorton Street

Carry on until the end of Lothbury and then stop and look straight ahead down the narrow, pedestrianised Throgmorton Street. The view of the clustered buildings along the north (left)

side is wonderful and provides a splendid impression of what the Victorian city must have looked like.

Now walk straight ahead along Throgmorton Street. On the left after about 100 yards (90 m), two giant bearded gentlemen hold aloft the grand pediment over the entrance to the Drapers' Hall, which stands on the site of Thomas Cromwell's mansion, taken over and sold to the Drapers by Henry VIII after Cromwell's execution in 1540. The entrance doorway is by T.G. Jackson, the architect of No. 2 Kensington Court (*see* page 70) and dates from 1898. The Hall has been remodelled several times since being rebuilt by Edward Jarman after the Great Fire, and the present remodelling is the work of Herbert Williams in 1868. If you get the chance to go inside look out for the Drawing Room, created in 1868 by Herbert Williams and decorated by interior designer John G. Crace, patriarch of the celebrated Crace family of interior designers, who worked on the interiors of the Palace of Westminster with Augustus Pugin and the Waterloo Chamber at Windsor Castle. To reach the Drawing Room you must first ascend the superb red and green marble staircase built in 1898 by T.G. Jackson.

Continue along Throgmorton Street. No. 26 (with XXVI carved above the door) is a mix of Italianate and Oriental design, the latter a nod to the building's owners, the Imperial Ottoman Bank. Built in 1871, it is the best known work of the architect William Cadell Burnet, who worked on the Law Courts with G.E. Street. Next door, at the junction with Old Broad Street, is a splendid five-bay Gothic building, with marble columns, carved stonework, a variety of pointed Gothic arches and a flurry of windows on the fourth floor. It was built in 1869 and designed by Thomas Chatfield Clarke (*see* Cornhill page 96).

☞ NOW TURN RIGHT INTO OLD BROAD STREET, LEFT INTO THREADNEEDLE STREET AND WALK UP TO BISHOPSGATE.

(18) No. 13 Bishopsgate

On your left is the tall arched doorway to No. 13 Bishopsgate, one of the City's most celebrated Victorian gems. Opened in 1865 and designed in neo-Classical style by Sir Charles Barry's assistant John Gibson as the new headquarters and banking hall for the National Provincial Bank, it was then the largest banking hall in Britain. The sculpted relief panels above the windows and between the Corinthian columns show the various industries and enterprises financed by the National Provincial Bank – agriculture, manufacturing, shipbuilding, mining, science and more – while the statues at roof level depict allegorical figures. Now called Gibson Hall in honour of its architect, No. 13 is used today for receptions, weddings and banquets. Have a look inside at the magnificent banking hall, which is lit by three glass domes.

☞ WITH GIBSON HALL ON YOUR LEFT WALK NORTH UP BISHOPSGATE, CROSS WORMWOOD STREET, GO ON PAST ST BOTOLPH BISHOPSGATE TO LIVERPOOL STREET RAILWAY STATION. TURN LEFT TO SEE THE EXTERIOR BUILDINGS AND THEN GO INTO THE STATION TO SEE THE VICTORIAN TRAIN SHEDS.

(19) Liverpool Street Railway Station
(1874)

Liverpool Street Railway Station was built in 1874 to serve as the City terminus for the Great Eastern Railway and was designed in fairly modest style by Edward Wilson. A rather more grand station had been planned but by the time the company had bought the land there wasn't much money left. The yellow-brick booking hall is simple Gothic. The two Victorian looking towers are fakes, put there when the station was restored in the 1980s, as are those by the eastern entrance from Bishopsgate. The red-brick Great Eastern Hotel to the east was designed by Sir Charles Barry in 1884 and extended further eastwards in 1891. The interior of the station was sympathetically modernised in the 1980s and the original train sheds restored to their full glory. The glass roofs are held aloft by slender cast-iron columns beneath iron brackets that burst out from the top like palm trees, while the two original naves or groups of platforms are divided by twin cast-iron columns. The view along the platforms resembles an avenue of waving trees and is quite lovely.

☞ RETURN TO BISHOPSGATE, TURN LEFT AND CONTINUE NORTH, WITH THE STATION ON YOUR LEFT.

Across the road and set back a little is No. 164, built as a fire station in 1885 by George Vulliamy of the architectural and clock making family, who rather specialised in fire stations, as well as being responsible for the sphinxes guarding Cleopatra's Needle on the Embankment. It is rather jolly in red brick with decorated stone facings and a splendidly elaborate pinnacled Dutch gable.

Carry on along Bishopsgate and cross the road at the lights to the Woodin Shades pub on the corner of Middlesex Street, bought by landlord William Woodin in 1863, according to a plaque on the pub wall, and rebuilt in its present form in 1893.

(20) Bishopsgate Institute
(1895)

Carry on up Bishopsgate until you reach No. 290, the Bishopsgate Institute, housed in an unusual late Victorian building showing elements of both Art Nouveau and Arts and Crafts. It was built in 1895 and designed by Charles Harrison Townsend, who was also responsible for the Whitechapel Art Gallery (*see* page 135) and the Horniman Museum in south London. The frieze above the wide doorway arch resting on truncated columns is decorated with Arts and Crafts style leafy trees, while the two turrets, which give the impression of raised arms, are embellished in distinctive Art Nouveau style. The building is narrow and looks as if it is trying to shoulder its way out of the row of houses that are squeezing it in.

☞ CONTINUE NORTH ON BISHOPSGATE UNTIL YOU REACH A CROSSROADS WITH TRAFFIC LIGHTS. TURN RIGHT INTO SPITAL SQUARE.

Almost immediately on the right, No. 37, with the red door, is the headquarters of the Society for the Protection of Ancient Buildings (SPAB), one of the very first conservation bodies, which was founded by William Morris and the architect Philip Webb in 1877.

㉑ Nos. 91–101 Worship Street
(1863)

☞ RETRACE YOUR STEPS AND CROSS OVER BISHOPSGATE AT THE TRAFFIC LIGHTS, TURN RIGHT AND CROSS OVER PRIMROSE STREET, CONTINUE NORTH ON BISHOPSGATE AND THEN TAKE THE NEXT LEFT INTO WORSHIP STREET.

We are now leaving the City for a brief foray into Shoreditch. On the right-hand side after about 200 yards (180 m) is a short row of most attractive Victorian shops with brown-brick houses above them, Nos. 91–101. The terrace was built in 1863 and designed by Philip Webb, architect of the Red House in Bexley and No. 1 Palace Green (*see* page 77 and SPAB, above). Webb usually designed individual domestic buildings but was asked to build this terrace of affordable artisan's workshops, shops and houses as a charitable commission by Lieutenant-Colonel William Gillum, a hero of the Crimean War and mutual friend with Webb of William Morris and the Pre-Raphaelites, all of whom were keen to encourage artisan crafts. The architectural style of the terrace is simple Gothic, but the pointed brick window arches and steep roofs are early signs of the Arts and Crafts style that Webb would later develop with Morris. Basement windows allow light into the workshops below while the large shop windows allowed the artisans to display their wares. The big dormer windows provided light for artists at the top of the house. There is even a Gothic drinking fountain at one end of the terrace to complete the Victorian good works theme.

 ## Wesley Chapel Lavatories
(1899)

☞ CONTINUE ALONG WORSHIP STREET, PASSING OUT OF SHOREDITCH INTO ISLINGTON, AND AT THE END TURN RIGHT INTO CITY ROAD. AFTER ABOUT 200 YARDS (180 M) YOU WILL COME TO WESLEY'S CHAPEL ON THE RIGHT.

Although the chapel is not strictly Victorian, having been built in 1778, it is well worth a visit as it was restored and refurbished by the Victorians in 1891 on the centenary of John Wesley's death. The original pillars, which were made from ship's masts and were donated by George III, were replaced by marble pillars given by every country where Methodism is preached. The baptismal font is Victorian, as is the stained glass. But simply not to be missed are London's finest Victorian lavatories, which were installed in 1899 and can be found through a door just inside the main entrance to the chapel and down a short

flight of stairs. Each of the eight cedar wood cubicles along one wall contains a rare 'Crapper's Valveless Water Preventer', made by Thomas Crapper – who did not, as many would have it, actually invent the WC but did much to improve it, not least by inventing the ballcock. On the rim of the china bowls are the words 'The Venerable', referring to the model name, while useful instructions can be found written on the ceramic hand pulls, 'Pull and Let Go'.

Along the wall facing the cubicles there is a row of eight red and black marble urinals made by George Jennings, inventor of the first public lavatories, installed at the Crystal Palace for the Great Exhibition in 1851 (*see* page 21). At the far end of the room are eight marble hand basins.

Everything is in working order and kept immaculate. The marble and mosaic floor gleams. Even if you don't think these are the most beautiful gentlemen's lavatories in London, which I do, then you cannot deny that they are the cleanest and best looked after.

The ladies' lavatories are more modern and not worthy of a special visit, but ladies may take a look at the Victorian gents discreetly.

Entry to Wesley's Chapel, the museum and the lavatories is free. They are open from 10am to 4pm Monday to Saturday.

On leaving Wesley's Chapel, cross over City Road and take the footpath directly opposite, through Bunhill Fields Burial Ground, historically favoured by Nonconformists and last resting place of John Bunyan, William Blake and Daniel Defoe. When you emerge from Bunhill Fields you will see the Artillery Arms pub in front of you. In Victorian times this was a notorious dive called the Blue Anchor and was famous for rat-baiting, which meant pitting rats caught in the surrounding fields against some unfortunate dog. Today things are a bit calmer and it is quite safe to stop here for refreshment.

23 Chequer Street wood paving

Go right and left into Chequer Street to see the last surviving section of wood paving in London, which lies across the road almost immediately as you turn into the street. Wood-paved streets were introduced in Victorian times and widely used since they were quieter and much safer for horses than slippery stone paving. The wood paving here was put down in the 1990s to replace an older section that had decayed. Quite why it was decided to preserve this section here is a mystery, but thanks to that decision we can get some idea of what many of the streets of Victorian London once looked like.

Continue on Chequer Street, past a typical three-storey Victorian school building, now apartments, and you will find yourself in a world of vast Victorian social housing blocks, all part of the Whitecross Estate built by the Peabody Trust in the 1880s. Turn left into Cahill Street and left into Dufferin Street to see the Dufferin Court Dwellings for Costermongers on your right.

(24) Dufferin Court Dwellings for Costermongers
(1889)

This block was privately built in 1889 as housing for costermongers who had been displaced by the Whitecross slum clearance and needed somewhere not just to live but to store the handcarts from which they sold their produce. The block was shoddily constructed and the builder William Kelleway went bankrupt, so Dufferin Court was eventually purchased by the London County Council in 1891 as part of the 1890 Housing of the Working Classes Act, thus creating one of Britain's first council estates.

Turn around and continue along Dufferin Street to Whitecross Street, well known in Victorian times for its market, which in 1861 boasted some 150 stalls. A popular food market still flourishes in the street on weekday afternoons.

 ## Cripplegate Institute
(1894)

Go ahead past the eighteenth-century Two Brewers pub into Fortune Street, walk to the end and turn left into Golden Lane. Just past Brackley Street on the right we re-enter the City and immediately on the right is the Cripplegate Institute, former home of the Cripplegate Foundation, which brings together various local non-profit organisations. Red brick with Portland stone dressings, the Institute contained a large hall, classrooms, conference rooms and a library, but since 1987 has been used as offices. It was built in 1894 and designed by Sidney Smith, architect of the Tate Gallery. The pediment high up on the top floors shows Education flanked by Science and Art. On the spandrels of the wide arch over the entrance doors Science is shown holding a speed governor for a steam engine, while Art sits before a Classical building and holds the bust of a child.

☞ NOW GO INTO THE TUNNEL UNDER THE BARBICAN AND TURN RIGHT ON TO BEECH STREET. AT THE END GO OVER ALDERSGATE STREET, STRAIGHT AHEAD INTO LONG LANE AND HEAD FOR THE COPPER-DOMED TOWERS OF SMITHFIELD MARKET IN FRONT OF YOU.

Smithfield Market
(1868)

There has been a market at Smithfield since at least the twelfth century and today it is London's largest and oldest meat market. The present market buildings, which cover some six and a half acres (2.6 ha), were built between 1866 and 1868 complete with underground railway sidings connecting Smithfield to Blackfriars and Kings Cross stations, and were designed by the City architect Sir Horace Jones, who also designed Billingsgate and Leadenhall markets. The walls are of red brick with Portland stone dressings, while the timber roof is held aloft by cast-iron trusses and windows at lower roof level let in the light. The market is divided into east and west by a Grand Avenue with vaguely Classical pediments at each end and there are octagonal copper-domed towers at each corner.

Smithfield Market was extended westwards during the 1870s, and to see these extensions leave the Central Market by West Smithfield which runs along it to the south. The modern building on the right replaced the Poultry Market of 1873, which burned down in 1958. Ahead, much neglected and rather overlooked since they are now disused, are the surviving General Market buildings of 1873. To the left, rising beyond a small triangular lavatory block, is the Red House, built in 1889. This was one of Britain's first purpose-built cold stores and helped to transform the way that meat could be packaged and sold. To the right is the old fish market. The buildings here are exquisite and together form probably the finest Victorian market complex left in Britain. They are due to undergo what I hope will be a sympathetic restoration.

☞ AT THE BOTTOM OF WEST SMITHFIELD, TURN LEFT
FOR HOLBORN VIADUCT.

(27) Holborn Viaduct
(1869)

Sometimes dubbed the world's first flyover, Holborn Viaduct is a triumph of Victorian engineering. It was built over six years between 1863 and 1869 by the City Surveyor William Haywood to bridge the valley of the River Fleet as part of a scheme to connect the City to the West End. Before it was built, the steep and winding descent into the river valley down Charterhouse Street and up Snow Hill was somewhat hazardous for horse-drawn carriages. The bridge crosses Farringdon Road at a skew and consists of three cast-iron arches with two pedestrian tunnels running alongside the road arch. At the same time subways were built underneath the bridge for sewers and other services.

The elaborate and beautifully decorated cast-iron superstructure is carried on granite pillars, and on top of the central outer pillars are bronze statues of, on the south side, Commerce and Agriculture by Henry Bursill and, on the north side, Science and Fine Art by Farmer & Brindley, who also made the four winged lions at each end of the bridge. Between 1882 and 1886 the lights contained in the six cast-iron lamp standards on the bridge were lit with electricity from the world's first public coal-fired electricity generating station, opened by Thomas Edison at 57 Holborn Viaduct in January 1882. The station also provided power for the surrounding private homes, including those of nearby Ely Place.

Access to the bridge from Farringdon Road below was provided by staircases housed in four Italian Gothic pavilions, one at each corner, built in Portland stone. The two northern pavilions were damaged by bombing in 1941 and demolished in the 1950s but were rebuilt to the original design in 2001 and 2014 respectively. Note the matching cast-iron balconies at third-floor level.

Holborn Viaduct was opened by Queen Victoria on the same day that she opened Blackfriars Bridge.

(28) Oldest Drinking Fountain
(1859)

Climb on to the bridge using the staircase in the north-east pavilion and turn left (east) on Holborn Viaduct. Go past St Sepulchre-without-Newgate and on the corner by the traffic lights you can see, set into the church railings, London's oldest drinking fountain, which was erected on Holborn Hill on 21 April 1859, then moved when Holborn Viaduct was constructed, and finally put back here in 1913. The fountain was paid for by Samuel Gurney MP, who set up the Metropolitan Drinking Fountain Association in 1859 to provide free, clean drinking water as an alternative to beer – many of the fountains were sited close to pubs. Over the next 20 years the association put up some 800 fountains across London, which could be used by up to 300,000 people a day. In 1867 the association became the Metropolitan Drinking Fountain and Cattle Trough Association and began to erect troughs to provide water for animals as well.

Across the road from the drinking fountain is the Viaduct Tavern, which opened in 1869 to celebrate the opening of the Holborn Viaduct. It is a fine example of a Victorian Gin Palace and retains many original Victorian fittings, such as mirrors and etched glass panels.

☞ NOW CONTINUE ALONG NEWGATE STREET TO ST PAUL'S UNDERGROUND STATION AND THE END OF THE WALK.

End of walks: St Paul's Station

Recommended Places for Refreshment

The Black Friar 174 Queen Victoria Street, EC4

The Cockpit 7 St Andrew's Hill, EC4

The Sugar Loaf 65 Cannon Street, EC4

The Globe 83 Moorgate, EC2

Woodin Shades 212 Bishopsgate, EC2

The Artillery Arms 102 Bunhill Row, EC1

The Two Brewers 121 Whitecross Street, EC1

The Viaduct Tavern 126 Newgate Street, EC1

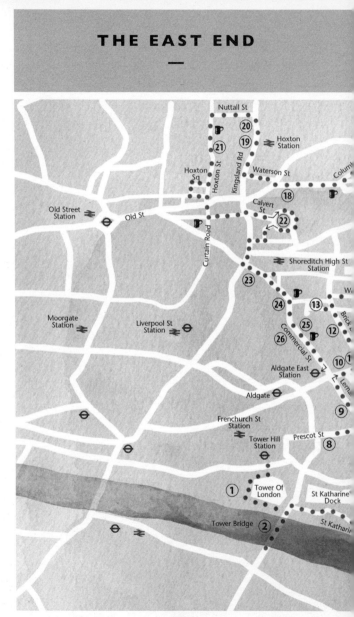

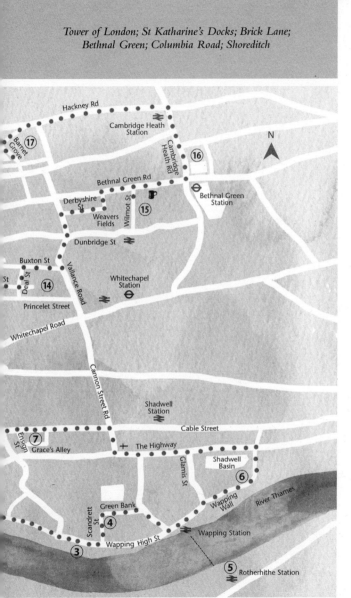

Tower of London; St Katharine's Docks; Brick Lane;
Bethnal Green; Columbia Road; Shoreditch

Hackney Rd

Cambridge Heath
Station

Cambridge Heath Rd

17

Barnet Grove

16

Bethnal Green Rd

Bethnal Green
Station

Derbyshire
St

Wilmot St

15

Weavers Fields

Dunbridge St

Buxton St

St

Deal St

14

Valance Road

Princelet Street

Whitechapel
Station

Whitechapel Road

Cannon Street Rd

Shadwell
Station

Cable Street

Ensign St

7

The Highway

Grace's Alley

Glamis St

Shadwell
Basin

6

Wapping Wall

River Thames

Scandrett St

Green Bank

4

Wapping Station

3

Wapping High St

5 Rotherhithe Station

Chapter 4
Walking in the Victorian East End

On these walks we visit the East End, London's historic industrial and dockland centre. During the Victorian Age, when London became the world's industrial capital, the area expanded rapidly and haphazardly, as London's docks grew to handle over half the world's trade and waves of immigration added to the overcrowding. Like the City, the East End was badly bombed in the Second World War but nonetheless we will see some of the earliest attempts at social housing and philanthropic enterprises as well as some good examples of pioneering Victorian engineering.

Numbers applied to each attraction refer to the numbers on the map

Walks

Start walking: Tower Hill Station

☞ EXIT TOWER HILL STATION, FOLLOW SIGNS FOR THE
TOWER OF LONDON AND MAKE YOUR WAY TO THE WEST
SIDE OF THE TOWER TO WHERE THE TICKET BOOTHS AND
ENTRANCE ARE LOCATED. JUST BEYOND THE SOUVENIR
SHOP IS ...

① **Tower Subway**
(1869)

The small round brick building here is the entrance to only the second tunnel dug under the River Thames, and the first tunnel in the world to be lined with iron rather than brick. Running for 1,340 feet (408 m) from Tower Hill to Tooley Street on the south bank, the Tower Subway was the world's first underground tube railway tunnel and was built in 1869 by tunnelling engineer Peter Barlow and his pupil J.H. Greathead (*see* page 98), using a revolutionary wrought-iron tunnelling shield patented by Barlow and developed further by Greathead. At first passengers were transported 12 at a time on a cable-hauled tram, but this proved uneconomic and so the tunnel was converted into a foot tunnel, which was used by over one million people a year. However, once Tower Bridge was opened in 1896 and people could walk over the river for free, Tower Subway became uneconomic and was closed. It was eventually sold to the London Hydraulic Power Company and is still used today for water mains.

Tower Bridge
(1894)

☞ NOW WALK ALONG THE RIVERSIDE TERRACE IN FRONT OF THE TOWER OF LONDON AND CLIMB THE STEPS UP ON TO TOWER BRIDGE, A VICTORIAN MASTERPIECE AND PERHAPS THE MOST RECOGNISABLE BRIDGE IN THE WORLD.

Officially opened by the Prince of Wales in 1894, the bridge was designed by the City architect Sir Horace Jones and engineered by Sir John Wolfe-Barry, youngest son of Sir Charles Barry. The famous Gothic towers, which are 213 feet (65 m) high, are basically steel frames clad with Cornish granite and Portland stone and are intended to complement the adjacent Tower of London. In Victorian times the high-level walkways, which are 143 feet (44 m) above the water, became a haunt for prostitutes and pickpockets and they were eventually closed in

1910. They were reopened in 1982 and lifts were installed in the towers for those who don't fancy climbing the steep staircase.

The side spans of Tower Bridge are suspension bridges, while the centre span is 200 feet (61 m) in length with twin bascules, or leaves, that weigh over 1,000 tons each. The raising mechanism for the bascules originally used hydraulics powered by steam engines, but in 1976 the system was switched to electric power while the hydraulic fluid was changed from water to oil. As the bascules open, vast counterweights descend into the space below that is contained within the great concrete piers at the base of each tower. When the bridge is closed these enormous chambers are left echoingly empty, forming two of the great hidden Victorian spaces of London. In recent years concerts have been held in the chambers. The Victorian engine-room at the south end of the bridge is now a museum, where you can see the steam engines, coal burners and accumulators that powered the bridge for over 80 years.

Tower Bridge was the first bridge to be built across the Thames below London Bridge, and because it gave access to the Pool of London, which was the busiest port in the world at the time, it was in constant use, sometimes being raised 50 times a day or more. Today the bridge is raised roughly 1,000 times a year.

☞ ON LEAVING TOWER BRIDGE, GO DOWN THE STEPS TO THE TERRACE IN FRONT OF THE TOWER HOTEL AND MAKE YOUR WAY ALONG THE RIVER TO ST KATHARINE'S DOCKS. GO ACROSS THE PEDESTRIAN BRIDGE AT THE RIVER ENTRANCE TO THE DOCKS, THEN LEFT AND RIGHT ON TO THE PINK-BRICK ROAD. FOLLOW THIS EASTWARDS PAST DEVON HOUSE AND OUT ON TO COBBLED ST KATHARINE'S WAY. TURN RIGHT AND FOLLOW ST KATHARINE'S WAY PAST ROWS OF CONVERTED VICTORIAN

WAREHOUSES TO THE END. TURN RIGHT INTO WAPPING
HIGH STREET AND CONTINUE FOR A QUARTER OF A MILE,
PASSING THE SPLENDID GEORGIAN HOUSES OF WAPPING
PIERHEAD.

③ Oliver's Wharf
(1869)

Just beyond the Town of Ramsgate pub is the deliciously
Gothic Oliver's Wharf, built in 1869 for George Oliver by
Frederick and Horace Francis to handle tea and other cargoes. In
1972 it became the first of Wapping's many Victorian warehouses
to be converted into apartments, and can boast amongst its
famous residents, past and present, actor Sir Alec Guinness, pop
star Cher and Dire Straits frontman Mark Knopfler.

④ St Patrick's Church
(1879)

Take the next left by Pierhead Wharf, into Scandrett Street,
then turn right into Green Bank by the Turk's Head,
famous as the last watering hole for condemned men on their
way from Newgate Prison to nearby Execution Dock, which
was where the new Thames River Police headquarters station
now stands. A little way along Green Bank on the right is St
Patrick's Roman Catholic church, built in 1879 for the many
Irish dockers in the area by F.W. Tasker. It is Classical in design
with a large round window at the west end, a feature of Tasker's
churches and, built on to the side, what looks remarkably like
the Tower Subway entrance but is, in fact, a small side chapel.

Inside there are tall Tuscan columns holding up the roof and the altar sits beneath a small vault. All very attractive.

☞ NOW CARRY ON TO THE END OF GREEN BANK, AND GO RIGHT, BACK TO WAPPING HIGH STREET, TURN LEFT AND WALK THROUGH THE CANYONS OF VICTORIAN WAREHOUSES UNTIL YOU REACH WAPPING STATION. HERE YOU CAN TAKE AN OPTIONAL DETOUR.

Optional Detour: Thames Tunnel
(1843)

Take a train from Wapping to Rotherhithe through the Thames Tunnel, the world's first underwater tunnel. The tunnel opened in 1843 and was built by Marc Brunel and his son Isambard Kingdom Brunel, who would go on to become one of the foremost engineers of the Victorian Age, using a revolutionary tunnelling shield invented by Marc. Although the tunnel was begun in Georgian times, it collapsed many times during the construction and was only finally completed thanks to Victorian engineering and technological know-how. It consists of two identical brick-lined shafts 1,200 feet (366 m) long, sunk 75 feet (23 m) below the surface of the river at high tide, and was originally intended for horse-drawn carriages. However, there was no money left to build the carriageway entrances at each end and so it was used as a foot tunnel. The tunnel was described as the 'Eighth Wonder of the World' and soon became the most popular tourist attraction in the Victorian world, with three million visitors in the first three months of opening in 1843. Eventually, just like the high-level walkways of Tower Bridge, it became a magnet for prostitutes and footpads and was sold to the

East London Railway Company in 1865 as part of the world's first underground system.

 ALIGHT AT ROTHERHITHE, AND AS YOU COME OUT OF THE STATION TURN LEFT AND LEFT AGAIN INTO RAILWAY AVENUE. ABOUT 100 YARDS (300 M) ALONG ON THE LEFT IS THE BRUNEL MUSEUM.

(5) Brunel Museum

The engine shed built for the steam-powered pumps that were used to extract water from the Thames Tunnel has been converted into the Brunel Museum, where there are displays about the building of the tunnel and further information about the Brunels, father and son, and their other projects. The enormous iron-clad shaft that served as a grand entrance hall to the tunnel has been restored, with a new oak and steel staircase replacing the Victorian stairs that wound around the walls, and forms another awe-inspiring Victorian space that demands a visit.

The acoustics are superb and the shaft now serves frequently as a concert hall.

Retrace your steps to Rotherhithe Station and return to Wapping on the train. When you alight at Wapping pause at the end of the platform before you go up the stairs as from here there is a superb view of the distinctive twin horseshoe-shaped tunnels of the world's first underwater tunnel.

6 Wapping Hydraulic Power Station
(1890)

☞ FROM WAPPING STATION CONTINUE ALONG WAPPING HIGH STREET, BEAR LEFT AT THE END AND THEN RIGHT INTO WAPPING WALL.

Opposite the Prospect of Whitby pub is the magnificent Wapping Hydraulic Power Station, one of five hydraulic power stations built for the London Hydraulic Power Company and the last of its kind left in the world, the others having all been demolished. It was built in 1890 to provide steam power for lifts, theatres and other machinery all over London, with steam sent through the Tower Subway for use south of the river. It housed six boilers and six pumping engines, with two huge accumulators for storing the hydraulic energy, and was fed by a vast underground reservoir that held 420,000 gallons. It was converted to electricity in the 1950s and closed in 1977, at which point it was the last working hydraulic power station in the world. The boiler house and engine-room were converted into a quite wondrous arts centre, with the machinery still in place, but the Wapping Project, as the centre was known, was forced to close when the lease ran out in 2013 and the property has been sold to a developer. Fortunately the buildings are listed and cannot be demolished, for this monument to Victorian engineering is breathtaking.

Hydraulic power was an important source of energy throughout much of Victorian London. It was used all year round, day and night, to power fire hydrants and cranes, to operate lifts in offices and homes throughout central London, to power factory machinery, to raise the curtain at the Royal Opera House, to open dock gates on the Thames and, most famously, to open Tower Bridge. In 1893 the London Hydraulic Power Company, with its main pumping station at Wapping, was pumping six and a half million gallons of Thames water around central London through 100 miles (160 km) of subterranean cast-iron piping. It was a brilliant system. In winter the water was kept heated, with the result that the roads and pavements above the pipes remained ice free. And once it had been used to power all that stuff, the water was simply returned to the river.

☞ CARRY ON ALONG WAPPING WALL, WHICH TURNS INTO GLAMIS ROAD, AND GO OVER THE BRIDGE ACROSS THE ENTRANCE TO SHADWELL BASIN WITH ITS GIANT RED-PAINTED BASCULE. CONTINUE ON GLAMIS ROAD AND TURN LEFT ON TO THE HIGHWAY.

TAKE A NO. 100 BUS OR WALK (15 MINUTES) ALONG THE HIGHWAY AS FAR AS THE CHURCH OF ST GEORGE IN THE EAST (ON THE RIGHT). TURN RIGHT PAST THE CHURCH INTO CANNON STREET ROAD AND LEFT AT THE END INTO CABLE STREET. AFTER ABOUT 500 YARDS (457 M) TURN RIGHT INTO ENSIGN STREET, JUST BEFORE THE TRAFFIC LIGHTS, THEN ALMOST IMMEDIATELY TURN LEFT INTO GRACES ALLEY FOR WILTON'S, THE WORLD'S OLDEST MUSIC HALL.

7 Wilton's Music Hall
(1859)

The only hint of what magic lies hidden behind the Georgian façades of the houses in Graces Alley is an iron gas lamp and a battered door of faded red paint with some worn stone carvings on the adjoining pillars. Wilton's began life as an alehouse in the early 1700s and by 1826 was known as the Mahogany Bar, because it was the first pub in London to have a bar and fittings made from mahogany. In 1839 a small theatre was built at the rear of the pub, and when John Wilton bought the place in 1850 he replaced the salon theatre with a music hall. It proved so successful that Wilton was able to buy up the rest of the properties in Graces Alley and expand into their back yards, where he put up a grand new music hall with space for up to 1500 people. It opened in 1859 and was described as '*the handsomest room in town*'. George Leybourne is believed to have given an impromptu first performance of the song 'Champagne Charlie', for which he wrote the lyrics, at Wilton's. After a bad fire, the music hall closed in 1880 and was taken over by the London Wesleyan Mission, who had little money to alter the place, which is one of the reasons why it has survived so remarkably untouched, enduring in all its Victorian glory as a large, dimly lit rectangular hall with a high proscenium arched stage and a gallery held aloft by barley twist cast-iron pillars. Unfortunately, the mirrors that lined the walls are gone. Today Wilton's is run by a trust and puts on plays, operas, concerts and readings.

☞ WHEN YOU LEAVE WILTON'S, RETURN TO CABLE STREET AND TURN LEFT, THEN RIGHT AT THE LIGHTS INTO LEMAN STREET. WALK UNDER THE TWO RAILWAY BRIDGES AND TURN SECOND LEFT INTO PRESCOT STREET, ACROSS

Wilton's Music Hall

FROM THE LARGE RED-BRICK BUILDING WITH THE CLOCK
TOWER ON THE FAR CORNER.

As you walk along Prescot Street, note the gloriously Victorian Princess of Prussia pub on the left, built in the 1880s. The equally glorious polychrome Venetian palazzo next to it at No. 16. is the former Whitechapel and County Court, built in 1859, and designed by the police station and county court specialist Charles Reeves and his colleague Lewis G. Butcher. The two buildings make a very splendid and evocative Victorian grouping.

Catholic Church of the English Martyrs

(1876)

Almost at the end of the street is the Catholic Church of the English Martyrs. This was opened in 1876 and was designed by Edward Pugin, son of Augustus Pugin, although Edward died

before the church could be completed, and it was taken on by his younger brothers Cuthbert and Peter. Like all the Catholic churches in this area it was built to serve the growing Irish population working on the docks. Two of the English martyrs to whom the church is dedicated are shown in the mosaic above the left-hand entrance door, Sir Thomas More on the left and John Fisher, Bishop of Winchester, on the right. Both were beheaded on nearby Tower Hill in 1535 on the orders of Henry VIII.

The interior is well worth seeing. The nave is short because of the constrictions of the site, and extra seating has been ingeniously provided by galleries on short, stumpy columns, while the tracery in the big Gothic windows (two of them rose windows) is superb.

⑨ Leman Street

 RETURN ALONG PRESCOT STREET AND TURN LEFT (NORTH) UP LEMAN STREET.

The red-brick and Portland stone building with the high clock tower across the road on the corner with Hooper Street was built in 1887 for the Co-operative Society by their in-house architect James Goodey, as offices and a tea warehouse. The name of the building, Sugar House, refers to the fact that it was built on the site of a sugar refinery.

Further up on the left-hand side is No. 70, The Oliver's Conquest pub, built in 1854 by Joseph Lavender. It was originally known as The Garrick Tavern after the first Garrick Theatre, which was attached to the pub at the back and was named in honour of actor David Garrick, who played Richard III at the Goodman's Field Theatre in next-door Alie Street in 1741. The manager of the theatre, which was demolished in 1889, was called Benjamin Oliver Conquest.

The Black Horse, on the corner of Alie Street, dates from the 1840s, while the Italianate building on the corner diagonally opposite is the former Eastern Dispensary, which was built in 1859 by G.H. Simmonds, a local surveyor who was also the Dispensary's secretary, with the help of voluntary donations. The Dispensary had been set up in 1782 by doctors working in the City and was one of the first meaningful efforts to provide medical treatment for the local poor.

☞ GO TO THE END OF LEMAN STREET, CROSS OVER WHITECHAPEL ROAD AT THE JUNCTION AND THEN TURN RIGHT ALONG THE NORTH SIDE OF WHITECHAPEL ROAD. ABOUT 100 YARDS (90 M) ALONG ON THE LEFT IS THE WHITECHAPEL ART GALLERY.

⑩ Whitechapel Art Gallery
(1898)

Built in 1898, the gallery opened in 1901 as one of London's first publicly funded art galleries. The clean, bold, unfussy design, breaking with all Victorian tradition, was by Charles Harrison Townsend and defies description, although there are strong elements of Art Nouveau and Arts and Crafts, as with his other works, the Bishopsgate Institute (*see* page 107) and the Horniman Museum. The huge round arched doorway is off centre with a symmetrical row of square windows above. As with the Bishopsgate Institute the twin towers give the impression of squat, chubby, upraised arms. There is decoration characteristic of Arts and Crafts at the base of each tower, while the blank wall between the towers was meant to carry a mosaic, but funds ran out.

Passmore Edwards Library
(1892)

The art gallery has now extended into the Passmore Edwards Library building next door, which was built a few years earlier in 1892 but might be from another age altogether. The library was funded by the newspaper publisher and philanthropist John Passmore Edwards but inspired by Canon Samuel Barnett of the local parish of St Jude's, who wanted to bring art and culture to the people of Whitechapel. He was also responsible for the founding of the educational establishment Toynbee Hall in Commercial Street. The library building itself looks to have been knocked around a bit but was designed to exude beauty and culture. It is a mix of Tudor and Baroque, red brick with a little Tudor tower, hard-wearing terracotta tiles to fend off the polluted air of the East End and a frieze of foliage at the first-floor level. The architectural combination with the very different art gallery

next door seems to work, although it is hard to imagine that the two buildings were built only three or four years apart.

 ## Christchurch Primary School
(1873)

☞ CARRY ON ALONG WHITECHAPEL ROAD AND AFTER THE LIGHTS TURN LEFT INTO OSBORN STREET. WALK TO THE END, CROSS OVER OLD MONTAGUE STREET AND GO STRAIGHT AHEAD INTO BRICK LANE.

On the left after a few hundred yards, just beyond where Brick Lane is joined by Fashion Street, is Christchurch Primary School, built in 1873 in a confined space in the graveyard area behind Christchurch by James Tolley and Robert Dale, architects of several East End schools. A flight of steps leads up to the classrooms on the first floor, above an undercroft originally used as a covered play area, but since filled in. The projecting block to the left of the stairs was the schoolmaster's house. The building is still used as a school.

(13) Princelet Street Synagogue
(1869)

☞ CARRY ON ALONG BRICK LANE AND TAKE THE SECOND LEFT INTO PRINCELET STREET.

Five doors down on the right, the house with the three round arches is No. 19. Behind the Georgian façade of this weaver's house, built by a Huguenot family in the eighteenth century, lies one of hidden Victorian London's most intriguing secrets: one of the capital's oldest synagogues. It was built out over the back garden in 1869 both as a place of prayer and a refuge at a time when Jewish immigrants arriving in the East End were still subject to persecution and poverty. The building is long and narrow, with balconies running along either side where the women and children would have sat while the men occupied the main body of the synagogue downstairs, and the whole space is lit by a long skylight of Victorian glass that stretches the length of the building. The balconies are lined with panels inscribed with the names of those who helped to fund the synagogue and include some well-known names such as Montagues and Rothschilds. The house is now run by the Spitalfields Centre charity as an exhibition centre and educational resource, telling the story of all the cultures that make up the area, but due to its parlous state the synagogue is open just a few times a year or for pre-booked group visits.

⑭ Victoria and Albert Cottages
(1858, 1864)

☞ CONTINUE ALONG BRICK LANE AND JUST BEFORE THE TRUMAN BLACK EAGLE BREWERY BRIDGE ACROSS THE ROAD TURN RIGHT INTO WOODSEER STREET, WHICH RUNS BETWEEN THE BREWERY WALL AND A GLORIOUS TERRACE OF VICTORIAN WORKER'S HOUSES BUILT IN THE 1850S – NOW HIGHLY DESIRABLE HOMES. CROSS SPITAL STREET AND CARRY ON ALONG WOODSEER STREET PAST THE MODERN FLATS UNTIL YOU REACH A DOUBLE ROW OF FINE BROWN-BRICK COTTAGES ON THE LEFT.

This is Albert Cottages, built in 1857–8 for poor artisan families. You will notice they have no front door on to the street, but turn into Hunton Street, just before the terrace begins, and look in through the small arched gateway in the wall. Access to the cottages is from this pavement that runs between the rows, and each cottage has a small front garden. A little way up the road on the right is St Anne's Church, built in 1855.

Carry on along Woodseer Street until you come to Victoria Cottages on the corner of Deal Street, an L-shaped row of cottages again reached from a pavement running between the rows. These were double dwellings for artisans and their families, one dwelling on each of the two floors, with three rooms and some sort of basic bathroom facilities. They were built by the Metropolitan Association for Improving the Dwellings of the Industrious Classes. Founded in 1841, this was the first of the Victorian associations to be created specifically to build affordable homes for the working classes, and was the forerunner of the modern housing associations.

Here in Deal Street in 1848 the Association had built one of the very first blocks of working-class flats, the Albert Family Dwellings, a five-storey block of simple, somewhat severe Classical design by the Quaker architect William Beck. They then bought up the surrounding land and built St Anne's Church in 1855 and St Anne's School in 1862, both designed by Gilbert Blount. Albert Cottages were begun in 1857 for poorer families who couldn't afford the more expensive flats in the Albert Family Dwellings. Victoria Cottages were built in 1864 and were designed by the Association's in-house architect Henry Roberts, a pioneer in the design of artisan housing, but also renowned for designing the Fishmongers' Hall by London Bridge in 1834.

The whole area was badly bombed in the Blitz and the Albert Family Dwellings were demolished in 1975, leaving only St Anne's Church, the school and the Albert and Victoria Cottages as reminders of this early experiment in affordable housing. The cottages, in particular, are a rare and precious example of the sort of worker's cottages that were once everywhere in the East End but are now virtually all gone.

☞ NOW WALK UP TO THE END OF DEAL STREET, PAST ST ANNE'S SCHOOL, TURN RIGHT INTO BUXTON STREET AND GO TO THE END.

Here there is an attractive L-shaped group of Victorian cottages with red bricks above the doors and windows. The social worker and philanthropist Mary Hughes lived in the house on the corner. Turn left into Vallance Road, go under the railway bridge and turn left at the lights into Cheshire Street. Almost immediately on the right is Britain's oldest boxing club, the Repton Boxing Club, established for East End boys by Repton

Public School in 1884 and now housed in a splendid Queen Anne style former Victorian bath house. Known as the 'Home of Champions', Repton Boxing Club has produced some 500 amateur and professional boxing champions including World Welterweight Champion John H. Stracey, Junior Middleweight Champion Maurice Hope and Olympic gold medal winner Audley Harrison – oh, and the club was also frequented by Ray Winstone, who won 80 out of 88 fights before he became an actor, and the Kray Twins.

Now retrace your steps to the traffic lights and turn left back into Vallance Road. Walk past Weavers Fields and turn right into Derbyshire Street lined with Victorian workshops and a delightful early Victorian terrace. Red-brick Oxford House at the end was built in 1884 as the first ever 'settlement house' where students and graduates from Keble College Oxford would come and live amongst the poor of Bethnal Green, giving lessons and organising youth clubs and other activities – Oxford House worked closely with Repton Boxing Club.

☞ TURN LEFT IN FRONT OF OXFORD HOUSE THEN RIGHT INTO BETHNAL GREEN ROAD AND THIRD RIGHT INTO WILMOT STREET.

Wilmot Street
(1870s)

The long unbroken terrace of five-storey Jacobean Italianate houses that lines the west side of Wilmot Street, and much of the east side at the northern end, was built from 1869 through the 1870s by the Improved Industrial Dwellings Company, which was formed in 1863 by the printer, banker and philanthropist Sir Sydney Waterlow, best known for leaving Lauderdale House and Waterlow Park in Highgate to the nation. The school on the left was built by the London School Board in 1873. Wilmot Street has been described as *'grim and canyon-like'*, but is far more attractive than some of the prison-like blocks that were being built for the long-suffering working classes elsewhere in the East End. Flats in the street today sell for up to a million pounds, and I doubt if even Sydney Waterlow himself could afford to live there now.

> ☞ Having admired Wilmot Street return to Bethnal Green Road and turn right. Go under the railway bridge and turn left at the traffic lights in Cambridge Heath Road. On the right after 200 yards (180 m) is the V&A Museum of Childhood.

 16

V&A Museum of Childhood

(1872)

In the late 1860s the iron sheds known as the Brompton Boilers (*see* pages 32–3) that had been built as a temporary home for the South Kensington Museum in Brompton (now the V&A) were moved here to Bethnal Green. They were encased in brick and terracotta tiles by James Wild and in 1872 the new Bethnal Green museum opened for the purpose of encouraging an appreciation of art and science among the working classes. For the first three years the museum displayed the Wallace Collection, then a variety of other collections until after the First World War when it opened a Children's Section. This expanded until in 1974 the museum became the dedicated Museum of Childhood. It is still an arm of the V&A.

☞ CONTINUE NORTH ON THE RIGHT-HAND (EAST) SIDE OF CAMBRIDGE HEATH ROAD.

On the right after about 200 yards (180 m) is all that is left of the famous Bethnal Green Hospital, a four-storey building in yellow brick with stone facings and a blocked entrance archway at the north end. The hospital opened in 1900 and this was the entrance block, containing the dispensary and various staff residences. The main body of the hospital was demolished in the 1990s and replaced with housing.

Running alongside the road on the other side are the brick arches that carry the tracks of the former Great Eastern Railway into London. They were built in 1870.

☞ WHEN YOU REACH CAMBRIDGE HEATH STATION, CROSS CAMBRIDGE HEATH ROAD AT THE LIGHTS AND GO STRAIGHT ON UNDER THE RAILWAY BRIDGE INTO HACKNEY ROAD. WALK FOR ABOUT A QUARTER OF A MILE UNTIL YOU COME TO WARNER PLACE ON YOUR LEFT. AFTER CROSSING WARNER PLACE, WALK PAST TWO PARADES OF VICTORIAN SHOPS AND TURN LEFT INTO NARROW COLUMBIA ROAD.

This leads to one of the loveliest, best preserved areas of working-class Victorian housing and shops that survives in the whole of London. Walk on past the Guinness Trust Building of 1862 on the left, the one surviving block from the Trust's only foray into the East End, and turn left into Barnet Grove. Walk along it, admiring the streets of Victorian houses to left and right, as far as Wellington Row, where two former pubs, the Prince of Wales and the Queen Victoria, with a coat of arms on the parapet, face each other across the road.

Jesus Green
(1868)

This triangular area of houses is known as Jesus Green and occupies land bequeathed to the Jesus Hospital Estate, a charity founded by James Ravenscroft in 1689. The present houses were built in 1862–8, by Henry Robert Abraham, architect of the world's largest cemetery, the London Necropolis, otherwise known as Brookwood Cemetery, near Woking in Surrey. The result is half a dozen streets of elegant mellow brick two-storey terraces, the best of their kind in London (Wimholt Street and Quilter Street are particularly fine).

Columbia Road

☞ RETRACE YOUR STEPS TO COLUMBIA ROAD AND TURN LEFT.

The south (left) side of the street is a long and beautiful terrace of plain and simple Victorian shops built in the 1860s at the same time as the houses of Jesus Green behind. The north side is a mix of houses, workshops and a school from the 1880s. Take a look at Ezra Street off to the right by the tiled Royal Oak pub for an example of an unspoiled late Victorian alleyway of little shops, warehouses and workshops.

On Sundays Columbia Road is transformed into London's largest public flower market, and is filled with colourful and delicious smelling flower stalls from end to end. Plants and flowers were first sold along here in the eighteenth century by Huguenot immigrants who lived in the area. They also sold caged birds, hence the name of the Birdcage pub on the left at the end of the row of shops.

☞ Bear right and continue along Columbia Road past the modern flats and housing estates.

The iron gates set in Gothic piers in front of the nursery school a little further along on the right are all that is left of the fabulous Columbia Market, a vast covered marketplace of 400 shops financed by philanthropist and banking heiress Angela Burdett-Coutts, the richest woman in England at the time and the first woman ever to be made a peer, by Queen Victoria in 1871. The market was designed in the style of a French Gothic cathedral by Peabody Estate architect Henry Darbishire and opened in 1869. The market buildings, which boasted a clock tower and a massive Gothic hall, were set around a central quadrangle and included accommodation for the traders above their shops, the idea behind the enterprise being to provide work and shelter for the area's costermongers and good, healthy, affordable produce for the local people.

Alas, a railway link from nearby Bishopsgate never materialised, while competition from established markets, such as Billingsgate – and the fact that the costermongers preferred to roam the open streets – meant that the market never took off. It was closed as a market in 1886, then became workshops and was finally demolished, amidst much anguish from early conservationists, in 1958. The site was redeveloped in the 1960s and is now occupied by the Sivill House tower block and the Dorset Estate.

It was Charles Dickens who encouraged Baroness Burdett-Coutts to redevelop the slums called Nova Scotia Gardens that had grown up here in the early nineteenth century, and along with the market she also built a large apartment block called Columbia Dwellings. This too, was demolished. Columbia Market's legacy lives on, however, with the Columbia Road Flower Market. Baroness Angela Burdett-Coutts was the daughter of the banker Thomas Coutts and at the time was the richest woman in Britain. She was one of the most generous of the Victorian philanthropists and became known as the Queen of the Poor.

Dominating the end of Columbia Road on the south side are the monumentally impressive, if somewhat grim, Leopold Buildings, constructed in an Italianate style in 1872 for Sir Sydney Waterlow's Improved Industrial Dwellings Company (*see* pages 141–2) by the company's builder Matthew Allen, who had developed the style in the 1860s and saw no need for architects in the building of such apartment blocks. The fact that these monstrosities have survived through nearly 150 years of neglect demonstrates that perhaps he knew what he was doing. The colour scheme of green brick, cream stone facings and dark red painted windows and doors is striking and really rather handsome.

☞ NOW FORK RIGHT AT THE END OF COLUMBIA ROAD, CROSS HACKNEY ROAD INTO WATERSON STREET, GO TO THE END, UNDER THE RAILWAY BRIDGE, AND TURN RIGHT. WALK UP KINGSLAND ROAD FOR ABOUT HALF A MILE, PAST THE GEFFRYE MUSEUM OF THE HOME, WHICH DISPLAYS ROOMS AND FURNISHINGS FROM HOMES FROM 1600 TO THE PRESENT DAY, AND ON YOUR LEFT JUST BEYOND A SHORT ROW OF VICTORIAN SHOPS IS THE ADMINISTRATION BLOCK OF THE FORMER SHOREDITCH WORKHOUSE.

(19) Shoreditch Workhouse
(1866)

The first workhouse was built here in the early eighteenth century but quickly became overcrowded and decayed and was redeveloped and expanded between 1863 and 1866. The red-brick and stone building we see here on Kingsland Road, now part of St Leonard's Health Care Centre, housed administration offices and some female dormitories and forms the main entrance to the site.

(20) St Columba's Church
(1867)

The tall, rather severe Gothic red-brick church of St Columba next door was built in 1867 to serve the spiritual needs of the workhouse inmates and was designed by James Brooks, who built several similar churches in the area. Brooks also designed the attached vicarage and school, which were added in 1873. The whole ensemble, while magnificent, has an air of Dracula's castle about it. It is now the headquarters of the Christ Apostolic Church.

 TURN LEFT PAST THE VICARAGE INTO NUTTALL STREET.

The west end of the church overlooks the hospital car park, and beyond, on the south side of the car park, are the workhouse dining hall and day rooms. In the south-west corner is the male accommodation block. Although some buildings have been lost, the view from the car park gives a good idea of what a typical Victorian workhouse and infirmary complex would have looked like.

☞ WALK TO THE END OF NUTTALL STREET PAST THE MODERN MARY SEACOLE NURSING HOME, WHICH STANDS ON THE SITE OF THE ORIGINAL WORKHOUSE, AND TURN LEFT INTO HOXTON STREET.

Here you will see the St Leonard Shoreditch Offices for the Relief of the Poor, dated 1863, from where the relief efforts were co-ordinated by the parish clergy.

Now continue south on Hoxton Street, past what was obviously once a fine Victorian pub called The Unicorn and a fine working Victorian pub, Howl at the Moon.

Hoxton Hall
(1867)

After about 200 yards (180 m) on the left is Hoxton Hall, one of London's two surviving early Victorian music halls, the other being Wilton's (*see* page 132). Hoxton Hall was opened as Mortimer's Hall in 1863 by builder James Mortimer, who wanted to create a place where the people of Shoreditch could come to enjoy music and educational entertainment, such as lectures illustrated by magic lanterns. In 1866 music hall impresario James McDonald took it over and the hall reopened as McDonald's Music Hall. All the major music hall stars appeared there and McDonald's Music Hall was such a success that the following year, in 1867, McDonald had to enlarge the auditorium, extending the rear balcony along both sides and adding an upper balcony by raising the roof. It is this 1867 auditorium design that survives today, remarkably unchanged. In 1871 McDonald lost his licence and the hall was purchased by Huntley & Palmers biscuit heir William Palmer on behalf of the Gospel Temperance Movement, and then it was passed to the Quakers, who were there for over 100 years. Just like Wilton's, which became home to the London Wesleyan Mission, Hoxton Hall escaped damaging redevelopment because it was occupied by an organisation whose role was to provide for the poor rather than spend money on their property.

Carry on walking down Hoxton Street. Opposite the Macbeth pub at No. 70, which was built in the 1860s by the Hoxton Distillery as a gin distillery called The White Hart, a plaque on the Arden Estate flats commemorates the 3,000-seat Britannia Theatre that stood on the site for 100 years from 1841 until it was destroyed by bombing in the Second World War. Charles Dickens was a regular visitor and he describes the theatre in *The Uncommercial Traveller*.

Continue down Hoxton Street almost to the end, and just before the junction with Old Street turn right into the largely Victorian Hoxton Square. In the north-west corner (opposite) is St Monica's Church and Priory, built in 1865 and designed by Edward Pugin. This was the first permanent Augustinian foundation in England since the Reformation. In 2013 a rare set of Pugin's original frescoes were discovered under layers of paint in the sanctuary.

☞ WALK ROUND THE SQUARE BACK INTO HOXTON STREET, TURN RIGHT AND THEN CROSS OLD STREET AT THE LIGHTS AND GO STRAIGHT AHEAD INTO CURTAIN ROAD. WHEN YOU REACH THE VICTORIAN BARLEY MOW PUB ON THE RIGHT, TURN LEFT INTO RIVINGTON STREET. GO STRAIGHT OVER SHOREDITCH HIGH

Street into Calvert Street, which leads to Arnold Circus.

Arnold Circus
(1898)

This is the garden heart of the world's first council estate, the Boundary Estate, which was built in the 1890s on the site of London's most notorious slum, Old Nichol. Soil and rubble from the demolished slum was piled up into a mound at the centre of the Circus and a bandstand was placed on top. It is still there.

The Boundary Estate was laid out between 1893 and 1898 by Owen Fleming (1867–1955), principal architect of the New Houses of the Working Class Department in the newly formed London County Council, and was opened by the Prince of Wales in 1900. The estate covers 15 acres (6 ha) centred around Arnold Circus, from where wide, tree-fringed streets lined with attractive red and white striped brick Arts and Crafts style apartment blocks radiate out. There are also schools, shops and workshops. The quality of the buildings was almost comparable to the mansion blocks being built in Kensington or Chelsea and was far superior to any public housing that had come before, setting the standard for subsequent council estates all over the world.

Having climbed to the bandstand at the top of the mound in the middle, return to Calvert Street and walk clockwise round Arnold Circus, past Virginia Primary School, which pre-dates the estate and was built in 1887 by Thomas J. Bailey, who specialised in these 'three decker' designs. Just before you get back to Calvert Street turn left into Navarre Street, walk down to the end and turn left into Boundary Street, after which the estate is named. Continue to the end, past Old Nichol Street, a reminder of the original slum, and turn right into Redchurch Street. You will then emerge into Shoreditch High Street opposite a typical Victorian Italianate building of the 1860s, now occupied by the NatWest Bank. Turn left, cross Bethnal Green Road, go under the railway bridge and turn first left into Commercial Street. Take the next left into Quaker Street to see the handsome red-brick Dutch gabled Bedford House, originally the Bedford Insititute, built in 1894 by Rutland Saunders on the site of the Quaker Mission House that gives the street its name. It is named in honour of the Quaker philanthropist and Spitalfields silk merchant Peter Bedford, who founded the Society for Lessening the Causes of Juvenile Delinquency, which was run from here until 1947. This beautiful building then became a warehouse for a while, but has been empty and neglected for decades despite several attempts by squatters and artists to renovate it as studios and living accommodation for local artists.

Commercial Street

Return to Commercial Street and turn left. The smoothly rounded Gothic No. 152 on the left with its multicoloured brickwork was built in 1861 by Ewan Christian as the Vicarage for the next-door St Stephen's Church, no longer there. Opposite, across the road, is a former police

station built in 1874, while at the end of the row containing the Vicarage, on the corner of Wheler Street, is the even more beautifully rounded and elaborately stuccoed Commercial Tavern, one of the few London pubs not to change its name since it was built in 1865.

 Peabody Buildings
(1863)

Next up on the right are the splendidly forbidding Jacobean Gothic Peabody Buildings, the very first model dwelling built by the Peabody Trust, in 1863. It was designed to fill a very awkward triangular plot by the Trust's in-house architect Henry Darbishire, who later built the Columbia Market up the road for Angela Burdett-Coutts.

The windows all boast a variety of white-painted arch, while the row of plain narrow windows at attic level indicate the laundry facilities and bathrooms, which filled the entire top floor along with an area for children to let off steam when it was wet outside. Each apartment had just one fireplace, in the living room, and no lavatories – these were located communally on the stairs.

Ten Bells
(1850s)

Further down on the left, across Hanbury Street, the red-brick No. 106 has a terracotta plaque heralding the entrance to Stapleton's Repository, established in 1842. Then two plain mid-nineteenth-century terraces ending at the Ten Bells pub, built in the 1850s and decorated inside with original Victorian tiling, the highlight of which is a mural on the north wall called *Spitalfields in Ye Olden Time – visiting a Weaver's Shop*, a homage to the area's weaving heritage. The mural was created in 1890 by the tiling specialists William B. Simpson and Sons, who provided – and still provide – the tiles for the London Underground. Two of Jack the Ripper's victims, Annie Chapman and Mary Jane Kelly, are believed to have been regular drinkers at the Ten Bells.

Spitalfields Market
(1893)

The west of Commercial Street at this point is almost entirely taken up by the buildings of Old Spitalfields

Market. The market was licensed by Charles II in 1682 as a fruit and vegetable market, and the gabled Queen Anne style market buildings we see here were built between 1883 and 1893 by George Sherrin for the market's last private owner, former market porter Robert Horner. A huge arch off Commercial Street leads through into the market square, which was covered by an iron and glass roof of lattice girders by Henry Lovegrove, the District Surveyor of Shoreditch, in 1893. Although the original wholesale market moved to Leyton in 1991, the old Spitalfields Market has become a tourist attraction in its own right and today there are stalls selling all kinds of produce, clothing and arts and crafts seven days a week, along with restaurants and shops.

Now finish the walk by continuing down Commercial Street to Aldgate East underground station. This next section of the street was laid out between 1843 and 1845, and many of the shops and warehouses that still line the road date from that time. Commercial House on the right-hand side, now a hotel, was built in 1858 as a Jews' Infant School. A little further down is a rather lovely yellow-brick Italianate warehouse of the 1850s, while on the corner across Wentworth Street is an ornate three-storey structure, originally built in 1850 as the Princess Alice pub and then rebuilt for Truman's Brewery in 1883. Go on past the modern Toynbee Hall, which replaces the Victorian hall founded by Canon Barnett in 1884, to the junction with Whitechapel Road, where you will find Aldgate East Station.

End of walks: Aldgate East Station

Recommended Places for Refreshment

Princess of Prussia 15 Prescot Street, E1

The Birdcage 80 Columbia Road, E2

Howl at the Moon 178 Hoxton Street, N1

The Barley Mow 127 Curtain Road, EC2

Commercial Tavern 142–144 Commercial Street, E1

The Ten Bells 84 Commercial Street, E1

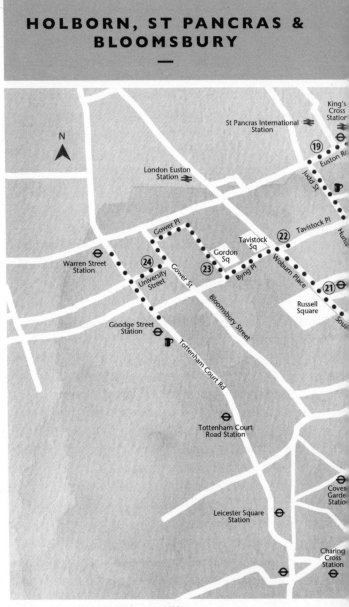

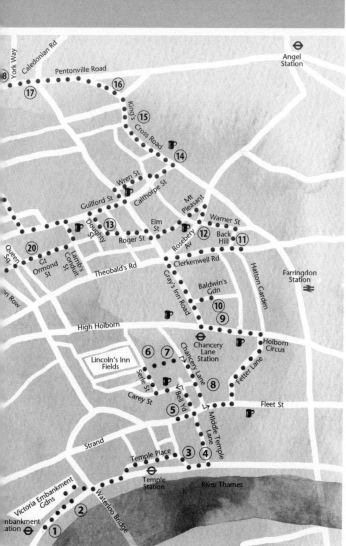

157

Chapter 5

Walking in Victorian Holborn, St Pancras & Bloomsbury

On this walk of contrasts we take in legal London, next a working-class area of slums that were razed by the coming of the railways and finally a fashionable area of literary fame that is home to many cultural, medical and educational institutions. Much of the Victorian architecture is of monumental size, and included on the walk are two of London's most iconic Victorian buildings.

Numbers applied to each attraction refer to the numbers on the map

Walks

Start walking: Embankment Station

① **Victoria Embankment**
(1864–70)

Exit station to Victoria Embankment, which was created in 1864–70 under the direction of Sir Joseph Bazalgette, necessitated by the need to provide central London with an effective sewage system. Throughout the Victorian era London grew in size and population at an alarming rate, and the amount of sewage and other waste flowing into the river made the Thames into a reeking open sewer. In 1858, during what became known as the 'Great Stink', a hot summer exacerbated the problem to the extent that the smell made it impossible for Parliament to function in the Palace of Westminster, despite the windows being covered with heavy drapes soaked in perfume, and at that stage the politicians finally decided something must be done. That something was the creation of the Victoria Embankment running between the Palace of Westminster and Blackfriars Bridge, along with the Albert Embankment running from Westminster Bridge to Vauxhall on the south bank and the Chelsea Embankment running from Millbank to Battersea Bridge on the north bank.

The work involved pushing out an embankment into the Thames, narrowing the river and making it deeper and faster flowing. Running alongside the river, behind the retaining wall, a sewage tunnel called the interceptor line was constructed to intercept sewage from all the other tunnels that had previously

drained into the river. The sewage was then sent eastwards to be dealt with downriver. At the same time, another tunnel was cut, inland from the sewage tunnel, for a new section of the District Railway running from Westminster to Blackfriars. The tunnels were then covered over to create a new riverside walkway and road, while the remaining reclaimed land was transformed into the Victoria Embankment Gardens. The system proved so effective that it is still in use today, virtually unchanged.

Cleopatra's Needle
(1878)

Cross Victoria Embankment (with the District Line running beneath) and turn left. Walk beside the river (along the pavement covering the sewage tunnel) as far as Cleopatra's Needle, which dates from 1475 BC and was a gift from the Turkish Viceroy of Egypt. It was brought to London from Alexandria and erected here in 1878. Buried underneath Cleopatra's Needle is a Victorian time capsule full of contemporary articles reflective of Victorian life, a copy of that day's *Times*, some coins, a copy of *Bradshaw's Railway Guide*, photographs of the 12 most beautiful women of Victorian England and a portrait of Queen Victoria. The sphinxes, which unusually look inward at the Needle rather than guarding it, were designed by George Vulliamy, nephew of church architect Lewis Vulliamy, as were the sphinxes on the arm rests of the benches along the Embankment and the delightful sturgeon lamp-posts on the walls.

In 1878 Victoria Embankment became the first street in Britain to be lit permanently by electricity.

Continue along the Embankment and cross the road at the next pedestrian lights into Victoria Embankment Gardens, where a little way along on the right you will find a memorial to Arthur Sullivan (1842–1900) who wrote the music to William Gilbert's lyrics for the Savoy Operas. Created by Sir William John, it was unveiled in 1903 by Princess Louise.

☞ LEAVE THE GARDENS AND FOLLOW THE PAVEMENT UNDERNEATH WATERLOO BRIDGE. AFTER SOMERSET HOUSE TURN LEFT INTO TEMPLE PLACE AND WALK TO THE END.

Astor House (Two Temple Place)
(1895)

The rather beautiful Elizabethan Gothic Portland stone building on the corner at Two Temple Place was built in 1895 by John Loughborough Pearson, regarded as the Father

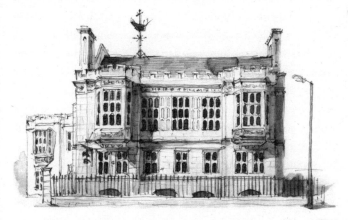

of Modern Gothic Architecture, to be the London home and offices of Viscount Astor, arguably, at the time, the richest man in the world. No expense was spared and it shows – this small but exquisite Victorian mansion is an architechural treasure. The exterior is decorated with stone carvings by Nathaniel Hitch, who also created a frieze for the interior of the Great Hall. This runs along the whole length of the first floor of the building overlooking the river and boasting, amongst other treasures, decorative panels by Sir George Frampton. The rest of the interior is equally ornate, with marble floors and fireplaces by Robert Davison, a mahogany staircase and panelling, exotic woodcarvings and friezes of characters from Astor's favourite novels executed by Thomas Nicholls, a close associate of architect William Burges. There is also stained glass by Clayton & Bell and what was then the largest strong room in Europe. Today, Two Temple Place, as it is now known, is run by a charitable trust as London's first gallery for showing publicly owned art from regions around Britain, and is open to the public during such exhibitions.

Across the road from Two Temple Place is the Temple Stairs Arch, built in 1868 as part of Sir Joseph Bazalgette's design for the Victoria Embankment.

Now turn left along the Embankment and you will almost immediately come to a pedestal with a silver and red painted dragon on top, one of a pair marking the boundary between Westminster and the City of London. The dragons, which appear on the City's coat of arms, were made in 1849 and originally stood outside the Coal Exchange in Lower Thames Street, one of London's first cast-iron buildings, which was shamefully demolished in the 1960s. Against the railings of the Temple Gardens here is a stone tablet with a relief of Queen Victoria, commemorating the occasion in 1900 when she was presented with the City sword by the Lord Mayor of London on this spot.

(4) **Temple Gardens**
(1880)

Now take the next left through the gates into Middle Temple Lane, which runs between Middle Temple on the west side and Inner Temple on the east side. The building straddling the arch across the entrance to Middle Temple Lane from the Embankment is called Temple Gardens and is the only building shared by Inner and Middle Temples. It was built in 1875–80 and designed by Edward Barry. Described as a *'vulgar monstrosity'* in its time, Temple Gardens is now considered *'exuberant'*. The stonework is certainly vibrant with decorative sculptures and carvings, most of them by Charles Mabey, whose work can be seen on the National Provincial Bank in Bishopsgate, now Gibson Hall (*see* pages 105–06). Flanking the archway in canopied niches are life-size statues of Learning and Justice by William Marshall, who also worked on the Albert Memorial.

Now walk up Middle Temple Lane to Fleet Street. Directly opposite as you emerge into Fleet Street is a building with Venetian windows and red marble columns. This was the Bank of England Law Courts Branch, which served the Supreme Court, built in 1888, and designed by Sir Arthur Blomfield, architect of the Royal College of Music. It is now a pub called The Old Bank of England.

Turn left. Immediately on the left is No. 1 Fleet Street, the home of bankers Child & Co., now part of the Royal Bank of Scotland. It was built in 1879 and designed in Renaissance style by the prominent bank architect John Gibson, of Gibson Hall in Bishopsgate.

The memorial in the middle of the road was designed by City architect Sir Horace Jones and marks the ceremonial boundary between the City and Westminster, the point where the monarch pauses to be offered the Sword of State by the Lord Mayor as a token of loyalty before entering the City of London. Jones's memorial replaced Christopher Wren's Temple Bar, which now stands at the entrance to Paternoster Square beside St Paul's Cathedral. The dragon, or griffin, on top of the pedestal was sculpted by Charles Birch. The statues lower down, of Queen Victoria and Prince Edward, the last royals to pass through Wren's gate, were the work of Joseph Boehm, who designed the head of Queen Victoria on the coinage.

⑤ Royal Courts of Justice
(1882)

Go to the second pedestrian crossing and pause to admire the Royal Courts of Justice, built in 1880 to bring all the great civil courts under one roof. The façade facing Strand is almost 500 feet (152 m) long, a truly spectacular ensemble of thirteenth-century Early English Gothic turrets and towers, pinnacles, gables and arches in brick and Portland stone that ably projects the full majesty of the Law. The Law Courts, as it is otherwise known, is probably one of the best-known buildings in London, constantly appearing on film and television as celebrities and others in the news are interviewed outside after a court appearance, and yet few people stop to appreciate this work of art in its magnificent entirety. This was the last great secular Gothic Revival building put up in London and has unfairly been called the 'grave of modern Gothic' – it certainly sent its architect, G.E. Street, to an early grave, the strains and pressures of completing this monumental work contributing to a stroke suffered while he was walking home from his local train station in Surrey at the age of 57. The building was completed by Street's son and Sir Arthur Blomfield and opened the following year in 1882. The interior is no less impressive than the outside with over 1,000 rooms and nearly four miles (6.4 km) of corridor. The Great Hall at the centre of the building, 240 feet (73 m) long, 50 feet (15 m) wide and 80 feet (24 m) high, with a vaulted roof, Italian marble floor and high Gothic windows, is one of London's great Victorian rooms. Against the wall close to the entrance is a fine memorial to G.E. Street designed by Sir Arthur Blomfield and sculpted in 1886 by H.H. Armstead, who also sculpted the artists, musicians and poets on the Frieze of Parnassus on the Albert Memorial. The Great Hall of the Royal Courts of Justice is truly a hidden Victorian gem.

When you leave the Royal Courts of Justice by the main entrance, turn left and then left again around the building into Bell Yard. The Court building seen from here is perhaps even more striking as the turrets and towers and gables and chimneys proliferate and soar in red brick and white stone.

At the end of Bell Yard is Carey Street. The Renaissance style building with the columns at No. 61 on the opposite corner was the Chancery Lane branch of the Union Bank of London, built in 1865 by the firm of F.W. Porter. It is even more grand at the front on Chancery Lane.

Now turn left into Carey Street to admire the back of the Law Courts. On the opposite side of Carey Street is a short row of interesting two-storey buildings including a delightful small Victorian shop front and the Seven Stars pub, a seventeenth-century building with a Victorian front and Victorian interior. Thomas More Chambers, the three-storey red-brick and Portland stone building at the end of the row, with the carved stone frieze and a statue of Sir Thomas More above the corner door, was built in 1888 by George Sherrin who, in his position as architect for the Metropolitan and District Railway, designed the Art Deco entrance arcade and platform canopies at South Kensington Station.

☞ TURN RIGHT PAST THOMAS MORE CHAMBERS INTO SERLE STREET AND THEN LINCOLN'S INN FIELDS.

⑥ Lincoln's Inn
(1845)

The east side of Lincoln's Inn Fields is dominated by the neo-Tudor Great Hall and Library of Lincoln's Inn, the biggest of the four Inns of Court, which also has the largest hall. Its Great Hall was designed by Philip Hardwick to replace the Inn's fifteenth-century Old Hall, which had become too small, and was opened in 1845 by Queen Victoria. The Library, also by Philip Hardwick, was built at the same time to the north of the Hall and was later extended to almost double the size by Sir George Gilbert Scott in 1872. To the untrained eye the buildings appear to be genuine Tudor and hence risk being overlooked by those seeking out Victorian London, but they are a superb example of Victorian architecture inside and out and should not be missed. In true Tudor style Hardwick's initials are picked out in stone high up on the south face of the hall. Highlight of the interior decoration is a huge fresco by G.F. Watts, entitled *Justice, a Hemicycle of Lawgivers*, which was completed in 1859.

To avail yourself of one of the frequent organised tours of the Hall and Library, enter the precincts of Lincoln's Inn through the neo-Tudor gateway at the south-east corner of Lincoln's Inn Fields by Serle Street. The gateway was designed to be all of a piece with the Hall by Philip Hardwick's son P.C. Hardwick, who worked closely with his father on the Hall and Library.

When you have visited the Hall and Library walk east towards the Old Hall and undercroft, with spacious New Square on your right. Go left and right around the Chapel, with its west bay of 1882 by Samuel Salter, to Gatehouse Court and use the Old Gatehouse exit into Chancery Lane, where you turn right (south).

(7) Chancery Lane

No. 33, a little way down on the left, is a Gothic red-brick block of 1874 by John Giles of Giles & Gough, architect of the Langham Hotel at the top of Regent Street. No. 87 on the right is a very pretty, tall and narrow Gothic house of red and yellow brick. Built in 1863 by Sir Arthur Blomfield, it is one of his earlier works and clearly influenced by William Butterfield.

(8) Public Record Office
(1851–91)

On the corner of Carey Street is the Union Bank building of 1865, already discussed (*see* page 167), while opposite is the former Public Record Office, now the Maughan Library, housing the main library of King's College. Begun in 1851 by

Sir James Pennethorne, fresh from laying out New Oxford Street through the St Giles Rookery (*see* page 214), the Public Record Office was built to bring under one roof all the national archives, government and court records going back as far as the Domesday Book of 1087, and was the first purpose-built fireproof building in England, equipped with fireproof storage cells and shelves made of slate. There was also a chapel and a reading room based on that of the British Museum. This was only the second large Gothic Revival building to be erected in London after the Palace of Westminster and is quite restrained, with just the turrets and towers hidden away at roof level giving away its more Gothic pretensions. What we are seeing on Chancery Lane is a later wing built by Sir John Taylor in 1891–6. Pennethorne's work faces Fetter Lane as we shall see later on the walk. The national archives are now housed in a new building at Kew.

Opposite the old Public Record Office, next door to Lewis Vulliamy's Law Society of 1831, is No. 114, the former office of Law Fire Insurance, which grew into what is now Sun Alliance. It has a Portland stone façade and Doric portico and was built in 1858 by Thomas Bellamy.

No. 115 next door is a yellow-brick building with a slightly over the top triple entrance, arched and decorated with carved stone faces. It was built in 1863 and designed by George Pownall. Pevsner dismisses it as worthless, which is a little harsh.

Nos. 123–126 on the right are mid-Victorian Italianate, while No. 193 Fleet Street, on the corner, is elaborate in red terracotta with columns and decorative carvings and a frieze above the first-floor windows. It was built in 1883 by Archer & Green for George Attenborough & Sons the jewellers, founded in 1843. The firm is still there, as is the original Victorian interior of custom-built Honduran mahogany and bronze. The terracotta pageboy figure in the niche above the door facing Fleet Street is Kaled, a character from Byron's poem 'Lara', and is a copy of Giuseppe Grandi's original sculpted in 1872.

Turn left into Fleet Street. Across the road the Barclays Bank building is by Sir Arthur Blomfield and dates from 1898, while the rather fun chocolate and cream No. 29 with its pink marble columns is by William Gibbs Bartlett of Brentwood.

Turn left into Fetter Lane, where you can get a good view of Pennethorne's wing of the old Public Record Office, and the square clock tower that was added in 1865. Follow Fetter Lane and New Fetter Lane up to Holborn Circus and cross Holborn at the lights. The statue in the middle of the road is a bronze of Prince Albert in a field marshal's uniform sculpted by Charles Bacon in 1873 and unveiled in 1874. It is the only bronze in London that shows an officer raising his hat in salute.

9 Prudential Assurance Building

(1879)

Turn left on Holborn and walk to the enormous red terracotta Prudential Assurance Building, designed by Sir Alfred Waterhouse, architect of the Natural History Museum, and built between 1879 and 1906. The red terracotta not only makes the building stand out from the more traditional stucco and Portland stone but is hard wearing against the polluted London air, while the grandeur of the building, with its turrets and spires and huge central tower, reflects the wealth and pomp of the Victorian insurance industry. The Pru, as it is affectionately known, sits on the site of Furnival's Inn, one of the Inns of Chancery, where Charles Dickens lived from 1832 to 1837 and where he began writing the *Pickwick Papers* and *Oliver Twist*. He married Catherine Hogarth from there in 1836 and their first child, Charley, was born there the following year in 1837.

Carry on along High Holborn. If you are in the mood for some refreshment at this point carry on along Holborn for 100 yards (91 m) to the Cittie of Yorke. There has been a hostelry here since the fifteenth century and the present building dates from the 1920s, but the glorious interior is laid out in Victorian style with lots of mahogany, cubicles, frosted glass and a high beamed roof.

After refreshment go back along High Holborn and turn left into Gray's Inn Road then take the first right into pedestrianised Brooke Street for the church of St Alban the Martyr.

(10) St Alban the Martyr
(1859)

Squeezed in by offices and mansion blocks off busy Holborn, St Alban the Martyr is an extraordinary building and comes as quite a surprise. How could anything so huge remain so hidden? The colossal west tower is of red and yellow brick with stone stripes and could be made from Lego. A slender staircase turret with a steep pitched roof ascends the west side of the tower flanked by two tall Gothic windows. The whole thing soars majestically out of the surrounding jumble. There is even room for a sweet little courtyard in front of the main entrance. St Alban was built in 1859 by William Butterfield, fresh from his triumph at All Saints, Margaret Street (*see* page 227), and very much shows his touch with colour and the ability to command a small, unpromising space. The inside is bright and spacious but, as with All Saints, the restrictions of the site mean that there is no east window, just a blank wall. The church was bombed in the Second World War but sympathetically restored by Andrew Gilbert Scott, grandson of Sir George Gilbert Scott. Fortunately, some beautiful stained-glass windows by Charles Kempe, which were installed in 1898, survive.

☞ RETURN TO GRAY'S INN ROAD. IF YOU WISH TO WALK THROUGH GRAY'S INN ITSELF, CROSS OVER THE ROAD AT THE PEDESTRIAN CROSSING AND ENTER THE INN THROUGH THE ARCHWAY OPPOSITE. WALK THROUGH GRAY'S INN SQUARE AND THROUGH THE PASSAGEWAY STRAIGHT AHEAD TO THE MAIN GARDENS KNOWN AS THE WALKS. TURN RIGHT INTO THE WALKS AND HEAD FOR THE EXIT ON TO THEOBALD'S ROAD AT THE NORTH-WEST CORNER. TURN RIGHT INTO THEOBALD'S ROAD AND WALK TO THE JUNCTION WITH GRAY'S INN ROAD.

OTHERWISE, TURN RIGHT (NORTH) FROM BALDWIN'S GARDENS ON TO GRAY'S INN ROAD, WALK TO THE JUNCTION WITH THEOBALD'S ROAD AND TURN RIGHT (EAST) ON TO CLERKENWELL ROAD.

Laid out in 1874–8, Clerkenwell Road was the central portion of a route between the East End and the West End of London. It cut through the slums that characterised the area, and vast blocks of social housing and model dwellings were erected along the route to house those whose homes were demolished.

Rosebery Avenue on the left was constructed between 1887 and 1892 to provide a direct route between Holborn and the

Angel Islington, and again huge apartment blocks were put up to house those displaced by the works. The vast, curving red-brick mansion block across the road at the beginning of Rosebery Avenue is one of those – Gray's Inn Buildings, built in 1887 by the Artizans, Labourers & General Dwellings Company.

The small two-storey building at the junction of Rosebery Avenue and Clerkenwell Road was built as shops in 1889 by architect and developer James Hartnoll, who in 1880 had built Cavendish Mansions, the model dwellings towering over them on Clerkenwell Road. Hartnoll was responsible for building many of the huge apartment blocks in this area, and although he worked for profit rather than philanthropy, his homes were considered much superior to those of the more philanthropic organisations because, amongst other things, they had their own individual lavatories and scullery.

☞ CONTINUE EAST ON CLERKENWELL ROAD, PAST THE CLERK AND WELL PUB ON THE LEFT, UNTIL YOU REACH THE PEDESTRIAN CROSSING AT THE JUNCTION WITH HATTON GARDEN ON THE RIGHT.

The brown-brick building on the corner of Hatton Garden and Clerkenwell Road with the pedimented front door is where Sir Hiram Maxim invented and first manufactured the Maxim Gun, the first recoil operated machine-gun, in 1881.

(11) St Peter's Italian Church
(1863)

A little further on along Clerkenwell Road, on the left, is St Peter's Italian church, built in 1863 to serve the Italian immigrants of Clerkenwell. It was designed by Irish architect

Sir John Miller-Bryson and modelled on the basilica of San Crisogono in Rome. At the time it was the only Roman basilica style church in Britain. Above the entrance are two mosaics showing the *Miracle of the Fishes* and *Jesus giving the Keys to the Kingdom of Heaven to St Peter*. Hidden away above the tall, pedimented façade is a brick bell tower that houses one of the largest bells in England, the Steel Monster, cast in 1862 by Naylor Vickers of Sheffield. If you can gain entry, the interior is splendid.

☞ NOW TURN ROUND AND GO BACK ALONG CLERKENWELL ROAD FOR ABOUT 50 YARDS (46 M) AND TURN RIGHT DOWN BACK HILL. GO TO THE BOTTOM OF THE HILL AND TURN LEFT INTO WARNER STREET.

(12) Warner Street Bridge
(1890)

Ahead, cutting through the huge, ubiquitous blocks of model dwellings, is the Warner Street Bridge linking the 14 arches of the brick viaduct that takes Rosebery Avenue over the valley of the River Fleet. Something of a hidden gem, this Victorian iron bridge, or flyover, is similar if somewhat smaller than the famous Holborn Viaduct and was designed in 1890 by Edward Bazalgette, who took over from his father Sir Joseph Bazalgette as acting engineer for the Metropolitan Board of Works (MBW). There is a staircase from Warner Street to Rosebery Avenue concealed within an arcaded brick pavilion incorporated into one of the apartment blocks.

Climb the stairs and then take a few minutes to wander along Rosebery Avenue in both directions to admire the work of James Hartnoll: to the left Rosebery Square in yellow brick, built

in 1890 as social housing, to the right Braunston, Barnstaple and Bideford Mansions, more for the middle classes in red brick with stone dressings and carvings and stepped gables, in the manner of Norman Shaw.

☞ GO BACK DOWN THE STEPS TO WARNER STREET, WALK UNDER THE BRIDGE AND TURN LEFT INTO MOUNT PLEASANT AT THE VICTORIAN APPLE TREE PUB, REBUILT IN 1872. WALK ALONG MOUNT PLEASANT, WHICH TURNS INTO ELM STREET BY HOLSWORTHY SQUARE, ANOTHER BLOCK OF MODEL DWELLINGS BUILT BY JAMES HARTNOLL IN THE 1880s. AT THE END OF ELM STREET USE THE PEDESTRIAN CROSSING TO CROSS GRAY'S INN ROAD, TURN RIGHT THEN NEXT LEFT INTO ROGER STREET. TAKE THE SECOND RIGHT INTO DOUGHTY STREET AND WALK TO THE DICKENS MUSEUM AT NO. 48 ON THE RIGHT.

Dickens Museum

This is Charles Dickens's only surviving London home. He moved here with his wife and first child from Furnival's Inn in 1837, just a few months before the start of Queen Victoria's reign, and while living here completed the *Pickwick Papers* and *Oliver Twist*, the first Victorian novel to have a child as the main character. He also wrote *Nicholas Nickleby* here. The young Queen Victoria was an avid reader of Dickens, *Oliver Twist* being a particular favourite of hers, and such was the overnight success of these early works that in 1839 Dickens and his family were able to move out of Doughty Street to a grander home in Devonshire Terrace just off the Marylebone Road near Regent's Park. The Doughty Street house, however, has been laid out as it was when Dickens was living there, with some of his original furniture, including his desk, leather armchair, portraits, tables, and some handwritten drafts of his novels. The house revolves around Dickens's study and provides an atmospheric insight into a typical early Victorian middle-class home.

☞ Upon exiting the Dickens Museum turn right and continue north on Doughty Street. At the next junction turn right on to Guilford Street then left at the lights into Gray's Inn Road.

The Calthorpe Arms, which is on the right after 100 yards (90 m), is a traditional Victorian pub set in a late Georgian building. In 1833 PC Robert Cully died in the yard of the Calthorpe Arms, after being stabbed during a riot by the National Union of the Working Classes in Coldbath

Fields, where Mount Pleasant sorting office now stands. He was the first Metropolitan policeman to lose his life while on duty in London.

St Andrew's Gardens, across Wren Street from the pub, were laid out in 1885 on the site of an old burial ground of St Andrew's Church in Holborn.

Turn right into Wren Street and walk to the end where it joins Calthorpe Street. The large yellow-brick warehouse buildings on your left look as though they could be surviving outbuildings of the Coldbath Fields Prison which stood on the site. The houses grouped around the triangle where the roads meet were built in the 1840s by Thomas Cubitt, one of the great Victorian house builders, whose vast builder's yard was nearby off Gray's Inn Road. No. 51 Calthorpe Street was a school.

☞ TURN LEFT INTO CALTHORPE STREET PAST THE
HOLIDAY INN AND THEN LEFT INTO KING'S CROSS ROAD.

Union Tavern
(1877)

Across the road is the Union Tavern, rebuilt in the Italianate and Gothic style we see today in 1877 after having been damaged by the building of the Metropolitan Railway through its back yard in 1865. The bar, with its wrought-ironwork and etched-and cut-glass screens, was created in 1891 and remains a good example of a traditional Victorian pub interior. Nos. 2 and 2a next door to the pub stand on the site of the pub's old brewhouse and were rebuilt in the 1870s at the same time as the pub.

(15) Old King's Cross Police Station
(1870)

Carry on north on King's Cross Road. Across Wharton Street is a row of three-storey terraced houses built in 1874, and then comes the rather wonderful, if somewhat forbidding, King's Cross Police Station, built in an Italianate style in 1870 on the site of a previous police station from the 1840s, which was demolished during the construction of the Metropolitan Railway. The Royal Coat of Arms above the door identifies the building as a police station and this was one of many Victorian police stations in London designed by the prolific police surveyor T.C. Sorby. The low building on the right of the police station was the cell block and contained eight cells. It sits right above the tunnel of the Metropolitan Railway, and the rail company had stipulated, when agreeing to sell the land back to the police after the construction of the tunnel was finished, that buildings directly above the tunnel should be of one storey only. The station, which in Victorian times was home to 100 police officers, still belongs to the police but today serves as a traffic warden centre.

The two-storey building to the left (north) of the police station, again with the royal coat of arms above the door, is all that remains of the previous police station and courthouse of the 1840s and is now part of the hotel that occupies the later courthouse, built in 1903 to replace the 1840s building.

Continue north on King's Cross Road, bear left by the Northumberland Arms and stick with King's Cross Road as it curves to the left. Nos. 112–126 form a row of eight houses and shops, six of yellow brick with round red-brick arches, the furthest two white painted, all built in 1886.

Cobden Buildings
(1865)

Next door, at Nos. 128–138, is Cobden Buildings, named after the free trade reformer Richard Cobden, whose campaign against the unpopular Corn Laws, which put tariffs on imported wheat and raised the price of bread, led to their abolition in 1846. He died in 1865, the year in which these buildings named in his honour were completed. This is the earliest surviving block built by Sir Sidney Waterlow's Improved Industrial Dwellings Company, which was founded in 1863 with the intention of ensuring that no working-class family should have to live in a single room, and the company's dwellings were amongst the very best of the social housing that was being built at that time, with individual wash houses and sculleries. They naturally proved very popular with the tenants. The company's first venture was Langbourn Buildings in Mark Street, Finsbury, now demolished, and they would later develop Wilmot Street in Bethnal Green and Leopold Buildings in Columbia Road. There were originally shops on the ground floor of Cobden Buildings – the fronts can still be seen – and the distinctive design of the block, with its central open balconies, thought to be the work of the company's in-house builder Matthew Allen, is replicated in the far larger Derby Lodge across the road in Britannia Street. Waterlow believed in putting the profits from his housing blocks back into the company, and Derby Lodge, which was built in 1870, was financed by mortgaging Cobden Buildings with the Public Works Loan Commissioners.

Further along on the right is the rear of the former Welsh Tabernacle of 1854, and then, where King's Cross Road meets

Pentonville Road, a block of shops and tenements built in 1883 by the developer George Ell. Turn left on to Pentonville Road and head towards the vast bulk of the glass-roofed St Pancras train sheds, which fill the view on the horizon.

(17) The Lighthouse Building
(1875)

Cross Caledonian Road and then York Way at the traffic lights to the square in front of King's Cross Station. Now look back at the 'flatiron' building at the junction of King's Cross Road and Pentonville Road to observe one of the mysteries of Victorian London. There is a lighthouse-shaped structure on the roof which dates from when the building was put up in 1875 and, since there is no light inside, no one knows what it signifies. There are many theories. It looks a bit like a helter-skelter, although this would seem unlikely considering its perilous position. A camera obscura? Investigations suggest there is not enough room inside. It may have been put there to advertise the oyster bar, the Victorian equivalent of a fast-food outlet, that occupied the building below. Or it could just be a Victorian folly. Whatever its purpose it is a conversation piece, which is probably exactly why it was put there.

(18) King's Cross Station
(1852)

King's Cross Station was built as the London terminus for the Great Northern Railway running between London and York, and sits on the former site of the London Smallpox

Hospital and, supposedly, the grave of Queen Boudicca. It was partially opened in 1851 to accommodate crowds coming to London for the Great Exhibition and fully opened in 1852, although Queen Victoria and Prince Albert left from King's Cross in August 1851 to travel to Scotland. King's Cross was London's fifth station and at the time was the biggest station in Britain and therefore probably the world. It is the work of Lewis Cubitt, younger brother of the master builder Thomas Cubitt, and you can tell it was designed by a builder rather than an architect because the design is simple, unfussy and effective, with the barrel-shaped glass roofs of the twin train sheds running over the concourse and through to the wide brick arches at the front of the station on Euston Road. The glass roofs, each with a span of 71 feet (22 m), were originally borne on laminated wooden trusses supported by brick arcades, but these were replaced by slender wrought-iron ribs in the 1870s. The front arches are separated by a clock tower, 120 feet (37 m) high, which has a hint of Venetian about it and perhaps presages the coming Victorian passion for Italianate architecture. The clock itself was made for the British Avenue of the Great Exhibition by master clockmaker Edward Dent, who would go on to make the Great Clock of the Palace of Westminster. The smaller arch to the right of the main arches marks the entrance to the original cab drive. To the west of the station is the Great Northern Hotel, which was also built by Lewis Cubitt and opened in 1854.

> ☞ NOW WALK TOWARDS ST PANCRAS STATION. THE MARVELLOUS VIEW OF THE STATION SIDE WALLS DOWN ST PANCRAS WAY TO YOUR RIGHT IS A GOOD APPETISER FOR WHAT IS TO COME.

⑲ St Pancras Station and the Grand Midland Hotel
(1868 and 1873)

Where King's Cross Station is beautiful in its simplicity, the Grand Midland Hotel that fronts St Pancras Station is spectacular in its extravagance, the finest station hotel ever built and one of London's two most iconic Victorian Gothic buildings (the other being the Palace of Westminster). Having been thwarted in his desire to build a Gothic building for the Foreign Office, architect Sir George Gilbert Scott poured his heart and soul into the Grand Midland, which opened in 1873. The hotel, as he puts it, *'is possibly too good for its purpose, but having been disappointed by Lord Palmerston of my ardent hope of carrying out my style in the Government offices … I was glad to be able to erect one building in that style in London.'* And what a building, born out of genius, driven by frustration and despair. Scott sketched out his designs while visiting his dying son, Albert, and one can see the manic intensity of his emotions in

the soaring spires and towers, dormers and gables and arches, and the brickwork patterns.

The glory continues inside, where Scott unashamedly highlights the strength and power of the structural engineering, making a feature of the granite pillars in the main rooms – they were made from 14 different types of granite and limestone – and painting the huge internal iron beams and their rivets so as to be an integral part of the decoration. The star feature is the majestic cast-iron Grand Staircase, which winds its way sinuously to the third floor, lit by tall Gothic windows and crowned at the top by a gorgeously painted stone vault with stone ribs and bosses. In May 1897 Scott's grandchildren climbed these stairs to say goodbye to their father, George Gilbert Scott Jr, also a brilliant architect, who died in one of the hotel's suites after bouts of madness and heavy drinking. In many respects the Grand Midland was the last word in luxury. It had hydraulic lifts, the first flushing toilets in any hotel in the world, the first public room in Europe where women were allowed to smoke, and the first revolving door in Britain, invented by Theophilus Van Kannel and installed in 1899. Guests who came to sample all this splendour included the music-hall star Marie Lloyd, Jesse Boot the chemist, George Pullman, creator of the railway sleeping car, and Cornelius Vanderbilt, the American railroad baron.

By the 1920s the Grand Midland began to lose its customers to more modern hotels as it lacked en-suite bathrooms, which couldn't be plumbed in due to the thick concrete floors that had been constructed for safety reasons. After several different uses the building was threatened with demolition in the 1960s but was saved after a passionate campaign led by poet Sir John Betjeman, a founding member of the Victorian Society in 1958. A statue of Betjeman stands inside the railway station that the hotel fronts.

St Pancras Station opened in 1868 and was built for the Midland Railway Company, who up until then had been sharing King's Cross with the Great Northern Railway. The Midland wanted a station – and a station hotel – to exceed all others, and they succeeded in achieving both. The incoming rail track had to be raised to pass over the Regent's Canal, so the platform deck sits some 17 feet (5.2 m) above ground level, supported by 688 cast-iron columns. The space underneath was used by Burton Brewers to store beer barrels. But it is the glass roof of the train shed, designed by W.H. Barlow and R.M. Ordish, that is St Pancras Station's crowning glory. Held up by wrought-iron beams that spring direct from the base of the brick side walls, at 100 feet (30 m) high, 240 feet (73 m) wide and 700 feet (213 m) long it was the largest single span in the world at the time and was copied everywhere, including at Grand Central Station in New York, built three years later in 1871. St Pancras was called the *'cathedral of railways'* and *'the largest and handsomest railway station in the world'*. Even today, especially as it has been superbly refurbished and restored as the terminus for the Eurostar, who could disagree?

☞ ON EXITING ST PANCRAS STATION BEAR RIGHT DOWN THE FORECOURT TO EUSTON ROAD. CROSS OVER AT THE LIGHTS AND GO STRAIGHT ON INTO JUDD STREET, DESCRIBED BY ANTHONY TROLLOPE IN *PHINEAS FINN* IN 1874 AS AN AREA OF *'DECENT AND RESPECTABLE OBSCURITY'*. GO ON PAST THE SKINNERS ARMS, FIRST RECORDED AS A PUB IN 1856, UNTIL JUDD STREET TURNS INTO HUNTER STREET AFTER THE CROSSROADS WITH TAVISTOCK PLACE.

Granville Mansions on the right is Edwardian, while the Royal Free Hospital School of Medicine on the left, originally the London School of Medicine for Women, was built in 1897 and designed in Queen Anne style by John Brydon, a Scottish architect who specialised in hospitals. He was a friend of Elizabeth Garrett Anderson, the first Englishwoman to qualify in medicine (she was also the first dean of the London School of Medicine for Women), and designed the Elizabeth Garrett Anderson Hospital in Euston Road for her in 1890.

☞ WALK ON DOWN HUNTER STREET AND CONTINUE
RIGHT TO THE END, PAST CORAM'S FIELDS (WHICH YOU
CAN ONLY ENTER IF YOU ARE ACCOMPANIED BY A CHILD)
UNTIL YOU REACH GUILFORD STREET. TURN LEFT AND
THEN RIGHT OPPOSITE THE MAIN ENTRANCE OF CORAM'S
FIELDS INTO LAMB'S CONDUIT STREET.

The Lamb, on the left, is one of London's most celebrated
Victorian pubs. It was actually built in the 1720s and refurbished
during the Victorian era. The interior is pure Victorian with
'snob screens' as insulation between bar staff and clientele.

Continue down Lamb's Conduit Street and take the first
right into Great Ormond Street at The Perseverance, originally
known as the Sun Inn and dating from early Victorian times. It
was a popular haunt of members of the Bloomsbury Group. Walk
along Great Ormond Street, noting the yellow- and red-brick
houses of Orde Hall Street on the left, which were built in 1892,
and go to the main entrance of Great Ormond Street Hospital,
marked by a glass canopy and blue-painted pillars on the right.
Follow signs to St Christopher's Chapel, which is just a short
walk from the entrance.

⟨20⟩ St Christopher's Chapel
(1875)

Described by Oscar Wilde as *'the most delightful private chapel in
London'*, St Christopher's Chapel was designed in glorious
pale red and gold High Victorian Byzantine by Edward Barry,
funded by his older brother William Barry, and completed in
1875. There cannot be another hospital chapel like it anywhere.

A painted dome is held aloft by four pillars of red Devonshire marble with gilded capitals, and there are murals, paintings and stained glass depicting childhood themes by the leading church decorators and students of Sir George Gilbert Scott, Clayton & Bell, founded in 1855. The floor is by Italian glass maker and mosaics expert Antonio Salviati (1816–1890), its design based on that of a pavement in St Mark's Square, Venice.

In the late 1980s, in an engineering feat worthy of the Victorians themselves, the whole chapel was encased in a waterproof box, lowered from the first floor to the ground floor and moved on hydraulic slides to its present position, while the hospital buildings around it were being demolished.

☞ ON EXITING THE HOSPITAL TURN RIGHT ON TO GREAT ORMOND STREET, GO ACROSS QUEEN SQUARE AND ALONG THE PASSAGEWAY PAST THE QUEENS LARDER PUB AND TURN RIGHT INTO SOUTHAMPTON ROW FOR RUSSELL SQUARE.

Russell Hotel
(1898)

Frightening the horses on the north-east corner of the once refined Georgian Russell Square, the flamboyant Russell Hotel, now called the Principal, is an unashamedly Victorian vision of a French château, a tumult of fairytale turrets and towers, chimneys and gables in streaky bacon stripes, arcades and bay windows, all picked out in tea with milk (thé-au-lait) terracotta and red brick. Four British queens, Elizabeth I, Mary II, Anne and Victoria, look down upon the main entrance as if to say 'now *this* is what a hotel should look like', and the hotel's four suites are named in their honour. The Russell Hotel was built in 1898 by Charles Fitzroy Doll, whose design was based on the fabulous Château de Madrid in the Bois de Boulogne in Paris, alas demolished in the 1790s. The rooms inside are resplendent, particularly the restaurant, which Doll was to recreate almost exactly for the grand dining room of the *Titanic*. Another connection is that the ship carried a twin of 'Lucky George', a bronze dragon that squats on a landing of the hotel's main staircase.

Doll went on to build another unrestrained hotel next door, the Imperial, but the square could withstand just so much exuberance – the Imperial was taken down in the 1960s and replaced with something more demure.

With the front of the hotel on your right, walk north into Woburn Place and take the second right into Tavistock Place.

(22) Mary Ward Settlement
(1897)

Almost immediately on the left is the rather marvellous former Mary Ward Settlement, perhaps London's finest Arts and Crafts building, certainly one of the first public buildings to be designed in the Free Style of the Arts and Craft movement. Built in 1897, it is the work of two young local architects, Cecil Brewer and Arthur Dunbar Smith, who won a competition judged by Norman Shaw. There is indeed a hint of Norman Shaw about it and also a whisper of Charles Townsend, he of the Whitechapel Art Gallery (*see* page 135). At first glance the front of the building is symmetrical, with the obvious exception of the huge stone

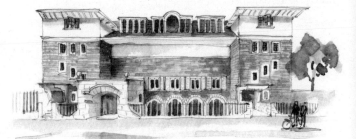

porch, but on closer inspection the symmetry dissolves – have a look at the positioning of the two identical side doors and the stepped windows above them. The front wall beneath the great overhang is free of ornamentation, and yet the east wall is adorned with a tree of life marked out in brick. Such details make this building never less than interesting.

Settlements were organisations set up by socially conscious individuals whereby young professionals and university students received board and lodging in a Settlement building in return for giving educational classes to the local poor. What became known as the Mary Ward Settlement was established in 1890 by Mary Ward, a best-selling novelist and the niece of Matthew Arnold, using rooms at University Hall in Gordon Square. The Settlement, which was modelled on Toynbee Hall in east London, became very popular and soon outgrew University Hall, and so the Settlement building here in Tavistock Place was purpose-built as a home purely for the Mary Ward Settlement. It was funded largely by the newspaper baron and philanthropist John Passmore Edwards. The Settlement moved to Queen

Square in 1982, and Mary Ward House, as it is called today, is now privately owned.

> ☞ NOW WALK BACK ALONG TAVISTOCK PLACE AND GO ACROSS WOBURN PLACE INTO TAVISTOCK SQUARE AND THEN GORDON SQUARE.

㉓ Church of Christ the King, Gordon Square
(1853)

Lurking in the south-west corner of Gordon Square is one of the finest examples of Early English Gothic Revival architecture in London, the Church of Christ the King. Designed by J. Raphael Brandon and financed by banker Henry Drummond for the Catholic Apostolic Church, of which he was a founder in 1835, the church opened on Christmas Eve in 1853. It is Westminster Abbey in miniature, and has the second highest nave in England, after the Abbey. Alas, the magnificent interior, with its hammer-beam roof adorned with angels, stone-vaulted sanctuary with brass lamp by Pugin, and glorious rose window by Archibald Nicholson, can be barely glimpsed from a lobby area reached through an arched doorway on the north side off Gordon Square, and the church is rarely open. Once the church of University College London, the Church of Christ the King is now home to the Forward in Faith Movement and is accessible to the public for a weekly mass or for the occasional organ recital.

Now walk north along the west side of Gordon Square. Next door to the church is the neo-Jacobean University Hall, built in 1848 as the first Hall of Residence for students of University College London. Walk on into Gordon Street and turn left into

Gower Place, lined with University buildings on the south (left) side, including a red-brick flourish at No. 23, built in 1850 and with a good Victorian shop front.

Turn left into Gower Street, where the Pre-Raphaelite Brotherhood was founded in John Millais's parents house (then No. 87, now No. 7) in 1848. On your left is University College London, where Charles Darwin had lodgings from 1838 to 1842 while researching coral reefs for his *On the Origin of Species*.

University College Hospital
(1897)

On your right, the frightening but enormously impressive red-brick Cruciform Building of University College Hospital could only be by Sir Alfred Waterhouse, who never designed anything less than gargantuan. Seven storeys high and shaped like an X with Gothic towers in each corner and at the centre, the hospital was built between 1897 and 1905, largely financed by Sir John Maple of Maple & Co., the furniture shop on Tottenham Court Road.

After the hospital turn right into University Street and then right into Tottenham Court Road for Warren Street Station or left for Goodge Street Station and the Victorian Rising Sun pub.

End of walks: Warren Street Station or Goodge Street Station

Recommended Places for Refreshment

Seven Stars 53 Carey Street, WC2

Cittie of Yorke 22 High Holborn, WC1

The Apple Tree 45 Mount Pleasant, WC1

Calthorpe Arms 252 Gray's Inn Road, WC1

Union Tavern 52 Lloyd Baker Street, WC1

Skinners Arms 114 Judd Street, WC1

The Lamb 94 Lamb's Conduit Street, WC1

The Perseverance 63 Lamb's Conduit Street, WC1

The Rising Sun 46 Tottenham Court Road, W1

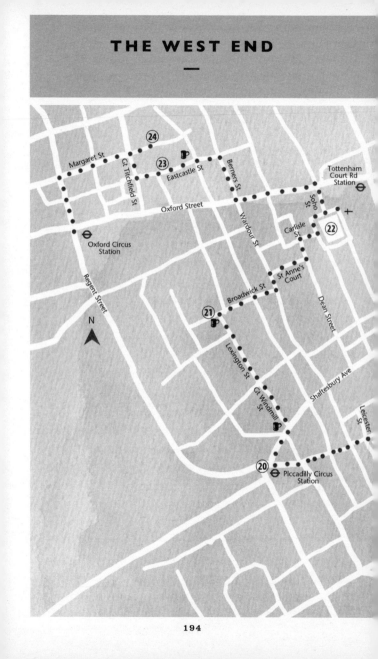

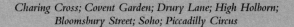

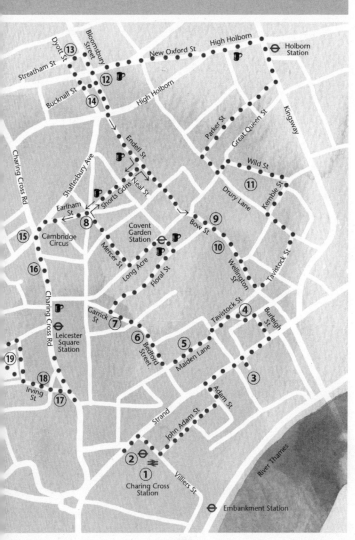

Chapter 6
Walking in the Victorian West End

These walks take in London's theatreland and shopping districts where the Victorians came to be entertained and to make their purchases. Much of the area was created by the razing of London's most notorious slums, such as the St Giles Rookery (*see* page 208), and some early examples of gritty social housing remain amongst the recreational architecture.

Numbers applied to each attraction refer to the numbers on the map

Walks

Start walking: Charing Cross Station

This leg of the walks begins on the concourse of Charing Cross Station.

① Charing Cross Station
(1864)

Charing Cross Station opened in 1864 as the London terminus for the South Eastern railway. It was built on the site of the Hungerford Market, a huge produce market that had been active there for 200 years but was badly damaged by fire in 1854. The station has six platforms, which were originally covered by an arched, single-span, wrought-iron and glass roof, and sits on a high brick viaduct. It was designed and engineered by Sir John Hawkshaw, who would later work on Cannon Street Station and parts of the London Underground. Hawkshaw also engineered the railway bridge, known as Hungerford Bridge, which replaced a suspension footbridge built by Isambard Kingdom Brunel in 1841 to serve the Hungerford Market.

☞ NOW WALK TO THE STATION FORECOURT AND LOOK BACK AT THE ...

② Charing Cross Hotel and Eleanor Cross
(1864)

The Renaissance style Charing Cross Hotel was designed and built, at the same time as the station, by Edward

Barry, third son of Sir Charles Barry, and is considered his best work. It was the first building in England to be faced with artificial stone, in this case provided by Blanchard's Manufactory. Blanchard's had been founded in 1839 by Mark Blanchard, an apprentice of the Coade Company. This company had invented the revolutionary Coade stone, a hard-wearing artificial stone used for the South Bank Lion at the eastern end of Westminster Bridge.

The Eleanor Cross was also designed by Barry, and was sculpted by Thomas Earp in 1863. The design was based upon the original thirteenth-century cross that had long stood at Charing, a hamlet on the bend of the River Thames where Trafalgar Square now is. It was the last of 12 crosses erected in 1290 by Edward I to mark the places where the body of his wife Queen Eleanor rested at night as it was brought back to London from Lincoln where she had died.

☞ NOW LEAVE THE FORECOURT, TURN RIGHT INTO STRAND, RIGHT AGAIN DOWN THE STEPS INTO VILLIERS STREET (FROM WHERE YOU WILL GET A GOOD VIEW OF THE CHARING CROSS HOTEL) AND FIRST LEFT INTO JOHN ADAM STREET.

On the corner of Buckingham Street, No. 22 is Italianate and quite lovely, yellow brick, rounded windows with red-brick arches and white-painted pillars and a delightful little gabled porch resting on pillars with ornamental capitals. It was built in 1860 and designed by Richard Pullan, brother-in-law of William Burges, the architect of Cardiff Castle and Tower House in Melbury Road (*see* page 53). Burges had his main office further down Buckingham Street and sometimes worked from No. 22 when he needed more space.

☞ WALK TO THE END OF JOHN ADAM STREET, LEFT INTO ADAM STREET AND RIGHT ON TO STRAND.

The Adelphi Theatre opposite opened in 1806, was rebuilt several times in the Victorian era, and in the 1840s was famous for putting on dramatisations of Charles Dickens's novels. The present building dates from 1930. The Vaudeville Theatre, a little further on, was opened in 1870 and the present façade, which is by C.J. Phipps, dates from 1889. The Victorian actor Henry

Irving came to fame here playing Digby Grant in James Albery's comedy *Two Roses* in 1870. The narrow red-brick house further along at No. 395 (now a souvenir shop), with arches and a pointed gable, was built in 1870 as a restaurant and then became a pub called The Irish House. Continue along the south side of Strand. The Coal Hole pub on the right occupies what was the Savoy Hotel's coal cellar in Victorian times.

③ Savoy Hotel and Theatre
(1881, 1889)

Turn right into Savoy Court. On the right is the Savoy Theatre, built in 1881 for impresario Sir Richard D'Oyly Carte as a home for the comic operas of Gilbert and Sullivan, which became known as the Savoy Operas. It was designed by theatre architect C.J. Phipps, who also designed the nearby Vaudeville and Lyric theatres, and was the first public building in the world to be entirely lit by electricity. The Savoy Operas were hugely successful and D'Oyly Carte built the Savoy Hotel next door with the profits.

The Savoy Hotel was designed by Thomas Collcutt, whose Queen's Tower still stands at Imperial College in South Kensington (*see* page 29–30), and opened in 1889. The original entrance was on the other side of the hotel off Savoy Hill by the river. Savoy Court and the present entrance were added by Collcutt in 1903. D'Oyly Carte wanted the hotel to compete with the best in America, and the Savoy was the first hotel in Britain to have electric lights and lifts, plus it had 70 bathrooms with hot and cold running water, one for almost every room. The first manager of the hotel was César Ritz, after whom the

Ritz Hotel in Piccadilly was named when it opened in 1906, and the first chef was Auguste Escoffier, from whom we get the word 'scoff'. In 1899 the artist Monet stayed at the hotel while painting the view of the River Thames from his balcony – alas the balcony is no longer there, the riverside front of the hotel having been remodelled in 1910.

☞ NOW RETURN TO STRAND, CROSS OVER AT THE LIGHTS AND TURN RIGHT IN FRONT OF THE STRAND PALACE HOTEL. AFTER THE HOTEL TURN LEFT INTO BURLEIGH STREET FOR ONE OF THE PRETTIEST AND MOST UNEXPECTED SMALL VICTORIAN HOUSES IN LONDON.

④ St Michael's Vicarage
(1860)

Standing out in red brick with stone dressings and decorated with yellow-brick diamonds, this delightful little house is squeezed into an L shape by its corner plot. It was built by William Butterfield, architect of All Saints, Margaret Street, (*see* page 227), in 1860, to serve as the vicarage for St Michael's Church, which stood opposite, where the Strand Palace Hotel is now. The church was demolished in 1906 and the house then became a clergy house for St Paul's, Covent Garden.

☞ GO TO THE END OF THE ROAD AND TURN LEFT INTO TAVISTOCK STREET.

The red-brick building with the arched windows across the road is the former Covent Garden flower market, built by William Rogers in 1871 and now home to the London Transport Museum.

St Michael's Vicarage

⑤ Maiden Lane

Go to the end of Tavistock Street and then left and right into Maiden Lane, once a small path running along the south side of what was then the 'Convent Garden'. In the 1870s the Duke of Bedford began developing the lane, after which it became the unlikely home at one time or another to many illustrious Victorians including Prime Minister Benjamin Disraeli, painter J.M.W. Turner and Prince Louis Napoleon.

On the left stands Corpus Christi Catholic Church, thirteenth-century Early English style with a square tower and a bit grim in brown brick, designed by Frederick Hyde Pownall and built in 1874. It was the first church in England to be dedicated as Corpus Christi since the Reformation. The interior is worth a look, a particular highlight being the altar, the work of Thomas Earp, sculptor of the Eleanor Cross at Charing Cross Station. A little further along, just after Bull Inn Court, a plaque by the stage door of the Adelphi Theatre informs us that *'William Terriss, hero of the Adelphi melodramas, met his untimely end out side this theatre on 16 December 1897'*. Matinee idol Terriss, one of the most popular actors of his day, was arriving at the stage door for that evening's performance of *Secret Service*, in which he was playing the hero Captain Thorne, when he was attacked and stabbed in the heart by Richard Archer Prince, an unstable actor who blamed Terriss for his own lack of work.

Next door, a rather shabby apartment block, withdrawn from the street, stands on the site of the house where J.M.W. Turner was born in 1775.

⑥ Bedford Street

At the end of Maiden Lane you will emerge into Bedford Street, home, at Nos. 39–40, of Britain's oldest women's magazine, *The Lady*, founded in 1885. The wonderful red-brick and terracotta building on the opposite corner (now

TGI Fridays) was built in 1877 for the Civil Service Supply Association, a co-operative department store. It was designed by Lockwood & Mawson, a firm of architects from Bradford who were responsible for Bradford Town Hall and the marvellous Saltaire, Sir Titus Salt's model mill town on the River Aire just outside Bradford. The CSSA building here stands on one of the two sites of Warren's Blacking Factory, where Charles Dickens worked as a young boy in 1824. Interestingly, Henry Lockwood of Lockwood & Mawson was the nephew of Charles Day, who founded a rival blacking company to Warren's called Day & Martin. Charles Day, who had lots of children, made a fortune from his blacking company and left a complicated will that was contested for years after his death, running up huge legal costs, a case that provided Dickens with the inspiration for the dispute Jarndyce v. Jarndyce in *Bleak House*.

Turn right up Bedford Street. Nos. 14–16 on the left were built in 1864, the middle one, No. 15, for Macmillans the publisher, who moved here from Henrietta Street just opposite. These houses were the work of Samuel Teulon, although the rather old-fashioned Italianate stuccoed look is completely at odds with Teulon's normal style of polychrome Gothic Revival. Next door Nos. 17–19, built as a District Post Office, was the work of two surveyors from the Office of Works, E.G. Rivers, who began the building in 1883, and James Williams, who completed it at the end of 1884. The style is High Renaissance. No. 25, now modern, was the London gallery of Goupil's Art Dealership, part owned by Vincent Van Gogh's uncle, and where the painter worked briefly in 1875.

☞ CONTINUE UP BEDFORD STREET AND BEAR LEFT AT THE TOP, WHERE IT BECOMES GARRICK STREET.

The shop facing you in King Street is the original Moss Bros store. Moss Bros was founded in 1851 by Moses Moss, who moved into the store here in 1881. When Moses died in 1894, his sons Alfred and George took over. In 1897 they began the clothes hire business for which they are renowned when a friend, Charles Pond, too impoverished to afford a suit, asked if he could possibly hire one for performing musical evenings at private houses.

(7) Garrick Street
(1860)

Garrick Street was laid out in 1860 as part of the Seven Dials slum clearance (*see* page 208) and so most of the buildings in the street date from that period. The palazzo first on the right at No. 2 (now Carluccio's) used to be the auction rooms of Debenham Storr and Sons, built in 1860 by Arthur Allom. Note the bearded faces on the headstones.

The large palazzo further down on the left is The Garrick Club. It was built in 1864, along with the two buildings of five bays either side, by Frederick Marrable, and the club moved in there from their previous premises in King Street in the same year. The Garrick was named after eighteenth-century actor David Garrick and founded in 1831 as a place where *'actors and men of refinement and education might meet on equal terms'*. Prominent Victorians who were members include the two most celebrated writers of the Victorian era, Charles Dickens and William Makepeace Thackeray, who quarrelled at the club and refused to speak to each other again until just before Thackeray died in 1863. Novelist and inventor of the pillar box Anthony

Trollope was also a member along with painters John Everett Millais and Lord Leighton, actor Henry Irving and composer Arthur Sullivan. The club's collection of theatrical paintings, including a portrait of Garrick by Johan Zoffany, is the most extensive in the world.

Across the road from the Garrick, at the entrance to Floral Street, and in sharp contradistinction to the palazzo, is a wonderful High Gothic building of ordinary yellow brick with red-brick bands and stone dressings. Built as a mission school in 1860, this was an early work of Sir Arthur Blomfield, architect of the Royal College of Music in South Kensington (*see* page 28). Note the rose windows in the two gables on Floral Street and the stone figure of Christ in the canopied niche at first-floor level to the side of the entrance.

Now walk up Floral Street. The white stuccoed building on the right after 100 yards (90 m) is the former British School, built in 1838 by E.H. Browne. The date 1860 above the door refers to when the building was given its new Italianate front by C.G. Searle, at the request of Charles Parker, surveyor to the local landlord, the Bedford estate. Note the rather attractive campanile above the door.

Continue along Floral Street and turn left into James Street between two Victorian pubs, The White Lion and The Nag's Head, the latter built in 1900 by MP and architect Sir Philip Pilditch.

☞ TURN LEFT INTO LONG ACRE AT COVENT GARDEN UNDERGROUND STATION, THEN SECOND RIGHT INTO MERCER STREET.

Amazingly, Nos. 3 and 5 on the left, Maidstone House and Tonbridge House, and No. 8 on the right, all red-brick and stone dressings with fancy Baroque pediments over the door, were apartment blocks built for artisans' homes in the 1880s.

⑧ Seven Dials

Continue along Mercer Street to Seven Dials, marked by a column in the middle of the circle. Seven Dials was at the heart of the St Giles Rookery, based around the church of St Giles, which stands at one of London's most important crossroads, St Giles Circus. Rookery was the term given during the eighteenth and nineteenth centuries to a slum area of poor housing, with overcrowding, lack of sanitation, crime and prostitution, said to resemble the chaotic nesting habits of squabbling rooks. The St Giles Rookery was London's most notorious. During the 1850s and 60s the Victorians embarked upon a vigorous programme of slum clearance throughout London, demolishing homes, replacing them with social housing and laying out new roads and railways, but the problem was so widespread and engrained that it took until well into the twentieth century for most of the rookeries to be disposed of.

Turn right into Shorts Gardens, the street to the right of The Crown, a late Georgian pub with Victorian decor. Walk along Shorts Gardens. Many of the warehouses along these streets, now containing shops and restaurants, were built between 1876 and 1886 for the brewers Combe & Co., who in 1787 bought the Woodyard Brewery that had been established here in 1740. In 1898 Combe & Co. was amalgamated with Watney & Co. and Reid & Co. to form Watney, Combe, Reid & Co.

☞ Cross Neal Street and at the next crossroads turn right into Endell Street.

On the left is a simple Gothic building of red brick with blue and yellow brick patterning and five Toblerone dormers, the central one with a rose window. Carved letters beneath the second-floor windows inform us that this was the Lavers and Barraud Stained Glass Works, built in 1859 by church architect R.J. Withers. Lavers and Barraud were much renowned for their stained glass and, rather appropriately, at the south end of the building facing on to Betterton Street, beneath a crow-step gable, there is what looks like a Gothic church window.

Now continue south on Endell Street, noting the Victorian Cross Keys pub on the right, built in 1849. Where the road jinks left and right we enter Bow Street.

9 Bow Street Magistrates' Court
(1881)

On the left just past Broad Court is the former Bow Street Police Station and Magistrates' Court, successor to the famous Bow Street Magistrates' Offices established over the road at Nos. 3 and 4 in 1740, and from where London's first professional police force, the Bow Street Runners, founded by novelist and magistrate Henry Fielding, operated. The Bow Street force was disbanded in 1839 when the magistrates were relieved of policing duties by the newly formed Metropolitan Police. The Bow Street Police station was the only police station in London to have a white lamp outside rather than a traditional blue one as introduced in 1861. This is because Queen Victoria didn't want to be reminded, every time she came to the Royal Opera House, of the Blue Room at Windsor in which Prince Albert died.

The new Magistrates' Court on the east side of the street opened in 1881 and was designed in rather stolid Palladian style by Sir John Taylor, the assistant surveyor for London. In 1895 Oscar Wilde was tried here for gross indecency and was kept overnight in one of the four cells.

(10) Royal Opera House
(1858)

Opposite is the Royal Opera House, popularly known as Covent Garden. The present Romanesque building is the third opera house on the site, the previous two having burned down in 1808 and 1856. It was designed by Edward Barry and opened in 1858 with a performance of Mayerbeer's *Les Huguenots*. The frieze behind the giant Corinthian columns of the portico, showing Tragedy and Comedy, and the statues either side, are by John Flaxman and are all that survived from the fire of 1856. Adelina Patti made her debut in the present opera house in 1861, while in 1892 Gustav Mahler conducted Wagner's *The Ring* here.

The iron and glass Floral Hall next door, designed to be in keeping with the other Covent Garden market buildings, is reminiscent of the Crystal Palace and was built by Barry for the market flower sellers. It opened in 1860, not long after the opera house, and is now incorporated into it.

Bow Street now becomes Wellington Street and the three large arches of No. 39, on the right, belong to the Covent Garden Flower Market, built in 1871 by William Rogers and occupied today by the London Transport Museum.

(11) Some Model Lodgings
(1881)

Take the next left into Tavistock Street, cross Catherine Street, and go to the end, where you turn left into Drury Lane opposite the instantly recognisable Victorian three-decker school buildings of St Clement Danes primary school. These 'Board' schools, which can be seen all over London, were built for the London School Board, an elected board that was established in 1870. The Board's main architects were E.R. Robson and T.J. Bailey, who both favoured the prevailing Queen Anne style of the time, hence the tall, narrow, white-painted windows. Every Board school had three storeys so that classrooms could be segregated, the ground floor for the younger children, the middle floor for boys and the top floor for girls.

Take the next right into Kemble Street in front of the vast yellow-brick Peabody Estate, designed by Peabody's favourite architect Henry Darbishire in 1881, and the fifteenth such Peabody Building. On the right, in sharp contrast, is Bruce House, built in 1905 to house 700 men, but nonetheless a rather more picturesque Edwardian version of a model housing block, Arts and Crafts in red brick and with the mansard gables so beloved of the London County Council architect William Riley.

☞ CARRY ON ALONG KEMBLE STREET AND TURN LEFT
INTO WILD STREET, WHERE THERE IS AN ENTRANCE TO

THE PEABODY ESTATE SO THAT YOU CAN WALK IN AND HAVE A LOOK AT THE INNER COURTYARD. THEN GO BACK INTO WILD STREET, TURN LEFT AND WALK ALONG IT WITH THE PEABODY ESTATE ON YOUR LEFT. AT THE END OF THE ROAD TURN LEFT INTO GREAT QUEEN STREET, RIGHT INTO DRURY LANE AND THEN FIRST RIGHT INTO PARKER STREET.

Here you can find the earliest of the London County Council's model lodging houses, Parker Street House, built in 1893 – or at least the façade of Parker Street House, which is being preserved, admirably, while new building goes on behind it.

Now go to the end of Parker Street, turn left into Kingsway and then left into High Holborn. The NatWest Bank at No. 212 on the left is Palladian and was built in 1854, while the Princess Louise, a little further on, is one of London's most celebrated Victorian pubs. It was built in 1872 and has a superbly restored interior (1891) with etched glass, wood panelling, individual private booths and 'snob screens' to preserve middle-class drinkers from the impertinent gaze of the working classes and bar staff. Even the marble urinals in the gents' lavatories are Victorian – and listed.

Further along on the left at No. 198, where the road forks, there is one of those wonderful Victorian frontages, with rows and rows of windows of all different shapes and sizes, and arches, columns on the ground floor and a couple of pedimented doors. Nothing special, but deeply satisfying, built in 1870. Next door is the old Holborn Town Hall, the eastern section built as a public library in 1894, the rest added in 1906.

☞ NOW TAKE THE RIGHT-HAND FORK, INTO NEW OXFORD STREET, WHICH WAS LAID OUT THROUGH THE SLUMS OF

ST GILES BY SIR JAMES PENNETHORNE IN 1847, AND
PROCEED ALONG THE LEFT-HAND SIDE. CROSS MUSEUM
STREET BY THE OLD CROWN OF 1851, THEN CROSS WEST
CENTRAL STREET BY THE LATE VICTORIAN BLOOMSBURY
TAVERN.

James Smith & Sons
(1857)

Cross Bloomsbury Street at the lights in front of you and at the end of the block, at No. 53 New Oxford Street, is James Smith & Sons, not only the world's oldest and largest umbrella shop but also London's best preserved high-class Victorian shop. The business was established by James Smith in Foubert's Place off Regent Street in 1830, and the shop was opened by Smith's son in 1857. It has hardly changed since and, along with traditional Victorian standards of service, retains its original Victorian mahogany shop counter, display cases and fittings, with lots of brass and black and gold lettering. James Smith was amongst the first to produce steel-framed umbrellas, invented by Samuel Fox in 1848, and umbrellas are still made to order on the premises in their basement workshop, along with bespoke walking sticks and canes.

Parnell House
(1849)

EXIT JAMES SMITH & SONS AND CROSS STRAIGHT OVER
NEW OXFORD STREET, THEN TURN LEFT AND CROSS
BLOOMSBURY STREET. TURN RIGHT AND WALK UP

BLOOMSBURY STREET. TURN FIRST LEFT INTO STREATHAM STREET.

A little way along on the right is Parnell House –'Model Houses for Families', as it announces above the door. Parnell House was built in 1849 by the Society for Improving the Condition of the Labouring Classes as part of the slum clearance of the St Giles Rookery, and was one of the very first model dwellings designed to offer healthier and more spacious accommodation to families who had been living crammed together in one room. Parnell House was, in fact, the very first multi-level domestic building in the world, another Victorian first, and set the standard for future model dwellings, including those of Sir Sydney Waterlow's Improved Industrial Dwellings Company (*see* pages 141–2). Each flat had a minimum of three bedrooms, and its own scullery, water supply, WC and fireplace. The architect was Henry Roberts, one of the first, most innovative and most influential of those sterling Victorian characters who were determined to improve the living conditions of the poor. In 1844, the same year as he was rebuilding London's oldest railway station at London Bridge, Roberts became Honorary Architect to the newly founded Society for Improving the Condition of the Labouring Classes and later became architect for the Metropolitan Association for Improving the Dwellings of the Industrious Classes.

☞ DO NOT GO STRAIGHT ON ALONG BAINBRIDGE STREET BUT TURN LEFT INTO NARROW, COBBLED DYOTT STREET, ONCE THE CENTRAL THOROUGHFARE OF THE ST GILES ROOKERY, AND CROSS STRAIGHT OVER NEW OXFORD STREET (THERE ARE LIGHTS TO YOUR LEFT) INTO THE CONTINUATION OF DYOTT STREET. GO LEFT INTO BUCKNALL STREET AND RIGHT INTO SHAFTESBURY AVENUE.

14 Central Baptist Chapel
(1848)

The yellow-brick building on your right, with the large rose window between twin towers, is the Central Baptist Chapel, built in 1848 in Romanesque style by John Gibson, who would later go on to build the National Provincial Bank in Bishopsgate, now Gibson Hall (*see* pages 105–06). The church was a project of Samuel Morton Peto, treasurer of the Baptist Missionary Society and a founding partner of the building firm Grissell and Peto who, amongst other projects, worked on the Reform Club, Nelson's Column and the Houses of Parliament. This, the 'cathedral' of English Baptists, was the first Baptist chapel to be built in such a highly visible position and to look so proudly like a church, rather than a house, reflecting the fact that Nonconformists or 'Dissenters' were now more accepted in Victorian society. Apparently, the Commissioners were at first reluctant to lease such a prominent piece of land to Peto, on the grounds that Nonconformist chapels were usually so dull, possessed of no eye-catching features, such as a spire. *'A spire?'* cried Peto. *'We shall have two!'* And indeed the church did originally have two spires, atop the twin towers, but they were taken down for safety reasons in 1951. The interior, which was refurbished in 1964, is well worth a look, and has a gallery supported on cast-iron columns.

☞ CONTINUE DOWN SHAFTESBURY AVENUE. GO STRAIGHT OVER AT THE LIGHTS AND BEAR RIGHT BESIDE THE SMALL TRIANGULAR GREEN WITH THE ELABORATE FOUNTAIN AT ITS CENTRE.

This is Princes Circus, and the splendid fountain is Queen Victoria's Diamond Jubilee Fountain, erected by the St Giles District Board of Works to *'commemorate the sixtieth year of the reign of Her Majesty Queen Victoria 1897'*.

Bear left and cross High Holborn at the lights. The Gothic building in front of you, yellow-brick with red-brick bands, is the former St Giles National Schools building, designed by Edward Barry in 1860 to cater for 1,500 local children. Go left and right into Endell Street to see the rather more attractive front of the building.

Two doors down Endell Street on the right is the Eglise Swiss, or Swiss Protestant Church, designed in 1854 in slightly debatable Palladian style by architect George Vulliamy, whose great-grandfather, clockmaker Justin Vulliamy, had moved to London from Switzerland in the 1730s and had been a founding member of the Swiss Church in London.

As you continue down Endell Street, note how many of the recognisably Victorian buildings have large archways leading through to backyards; No. 61, for instance, was Latchford's Timber Yard. The modern flats on the other side of the road replaced the old St Giles Workhouse of 1879.

☞ CONTINUE DOWN ENDELL STREET, TURN RIGHT INTO SHORTS GARDENS AND FOLLOW THE ROAD THROUGH TO SEVEN DIALS, THEN TAKE EARLHAM STREET (THE FOURTH EXIT CLOCKWISE) TO SHAFTESBURY AVENUE.

⑮ Palace Theatre
(1891)

Left is Cambridge Circus, meeting place of Charing Cross Road and Shaftesbury Avenue. Both roads cut through the St Giles slums in 1887, laid out to a plan by the ubiquitous George Vulliamy and engineered by Sir Joseph Bazalgette. Cambridge Circus is named after Queen Victoria's cousin (and grandson of George III) the 2nd Duke of Cambridge, who declared Charing Cross Road open in 1887. It is dominated by the gargantuan Palace Theatre, which opened in 1891 as the Royal English Opera House with *Ivanhoe*, an opera by Sir Arthur Sullivan, which made a loss. After a second loss-making opera, the theatre closed a year later and reopened as the Theatre of Varieties, finally settling on plain old Palace Theatre in 1924. It was built originally for the impresario Sir Richard D'Oyly Carte and was designed by his favourite architect Thomas Collcutt, architect of the Savoy Hotel.

⑯ Charing Cross Road

After admiring the Palace Theatre from Cambridge Circus turn left (south) down Charing Cross Road, for the former Welsh Presbyterian Church, which is the scary-looking 'white' brick building on the right with the Norman arches and octagonal dome. This was built by James Cubitt in 1888 for the Welsh Calvinist Methodists, who would not have approved of the nightclub it became 100 years later in the 1980s, the Limelight. After a brief period as an Australian restaurant and then a squat, the church is now having its interior, and dignity, restored by the arts organisation Stone Nest, who are turning it into a performance space.

Carry on down Charing Cross Road, which is overlooked on the left (east) side by the massive bulk of Sandringham Buildings,

Welsh Presbyterian Church

opened in 1884 as social housing for 900 people displaced by the construction of Shaftesbury Avenue. The Porcupine, a Victorian pub on the corner of Great Newport Street, was first listed as a pub in 1873.

The elaborate, rose-tinted London Hippodrome, opposite, on the corner of Cranbourn Street, was designed by the great theatre architect Frank Matcham, who also designed the London Palladium, and opened in 1900 as a venue for circus and variety acts, hippodrome meaning an arena for equestrian or other sporting events involving animals. The first show performed there was a musical revue called *Giddy Ostend*, in which a young Charlie Chaplin appeared in one of his earliest roles.

Wyndham's Theatre, on the left, was designed by W.G.R. Sprague, a protégé of Frank Matcham's, for the actor/manager

Charles Wyndham and opened in 1899. The Georgian Bear and Staff was a favourite haunt of Charlie Chaplin while he was appearing at the Hippodrome. Further along on the left is the Garrick Theatre, built in 1889 by C.J. Phipps, architect of the Savoy and Vaudeville Theatres. The Classical building of Portland stone beyond, which curves away to the left along with the road, is the Old Westminster City Hall, designed by Robert Walker in 1890 and enlarged in1902.

(17) National Portrait Gallery
(1896)

Across the street, the rather fine Italian Renaissance building facing back up Charing Cross Road is the National Portrait Gallery, opened in 1896, funded by the philanthropist William Henry Alexander and designed by Ewan Christian. It was built specifically to house the growing

collection of the world's first portrait gallery, which had been established in 1856 to form a *'gallery of the portraits of the most eminent persons in British history'*. The statue outside is of the great Victorian actor Sir Henry Irving (1836–1905), the first actor to be knighted.

 The Beefsteak Club
(1895)

Now turn right into Irving Street, which rather happily takes its name from the aforementioned Henry Irving, but used to be called Green Street in respect of the bowling green that once existed on the site. The road was widened in the 1890s to make it easier to access Leicester Square from the new Charing Cross Road, and the buildings lining the street on the north side were demolished. They were rebuilt further back between 1895 and 1897 and most of the buildings date from this period. Perhaps the most interesting address in the street is No. 9, a tall, narrow, Jacobean style house with a forbidding black door. This is the unlikely home of London's most exclusive gentleman's dining club, the Beefsteak Club, founded in the eighteenth century, re-established in 1876 and moved to Irving Street in 1896. The premises were built the previous year by theatre and cinema designer Frank Verity. Although the club now has several hundred members, it has just the one dining room, a panelled, cream-painted room on the first floor of No. 9 overlooking Charing Cross Road, above an art shop. You can see the dining room's large Jacobean window from the road. Henry Irving was a member, as was the librettist W.S. Gilbert, as well as numerous dukes, earls, lawyers and politicians. Still today beef steak is always on the menu and all the waiters are called Charles.

Leicester Square
(1874)

Walk along Irving Street into Leicester Square, originally Leicester Fields, open land to the south of Leicester House that was laid out as a square by the Earl of Leicester in 1670. In 1874 the square was purchased by the notorious Baron Grant (*see* page 69), who laid out the gardens and gifted the square to the people of London.

In later Victorian times hotels and theatres began to replace the private houses that had until then lined the square, and the area became known for entertainments, and oyster bars. The Odeon cinema on the east side stands on the site of the Alhambra Palace, much visited by Queen Victoria, which opened in 1856 and was demolished in 1936, while the Empire Theatre on the north side was opened in 1884 and converted into a cinema in 1927. Next door is the Baroque Queen's House, built in 1897 as a hotel by Saville and Martin, better known for their pubs, while next door to that is the terracotta Victory House, built by theatre architect Walter Emden as the Grand Hotel and Brasserie de l'Europe in 1899.

From Irving Street at the south-east corner of Leicester Square walk diagonally through the square past the marble statue of William Shakespeare at the centre, which was erected as part of Baron Grant's renovations in 1874. It is the work of Italian sculptor Giovanni Fontana and was based on Peter Scheemaker's Shakespeare memorial in Poet's Corner in Westminster Abbey.

On arriving at the north-west corner of the square turn left. As you do, look right up Leicester Street to see the unusual Bavarian style big step gable of the former St John's Hospital, designed by theatre designer Frank Verity in 1897.

(20) Piccadilly Circus

Cross Wardour Street into Coventry Street and head towards Piccadilly Circus, crossing Rupert Street and then Great Windmill Street. On your right is the former London Pavilion, originally built as a music hall in 1861. The term jingoism, meaning aggressive nationalism, originates from an anti-Russian song performed here in 1878 during the Russo-Turkish war, that went, *'We don't want to fight but by Jingo if we do / We've got the ships, we've got the men, we've got the money too ...'*

The Pavilion was rebuilt in its present Classical form in 1885 by James Saunders and Robert Worley as a variety theatre. The interior has been reconstructed many times since then, but the 1885 façade has been retained.

Now cross over at the lights to Piccadilly Circus and the statue of Eros at the centre. Unveiled in 1893 as a tribute to the philanthropist and reformer Lord Shaftesbury, this was the first aluminium statue in the world. It was the work of Sir Alfred Gilbert and actually represents the Angel of Christian Charity, but since the statue was near nude and carried a bow and arrow it was nicknamed Eros and the name stuck.

The Criterion Theatre and Restaurant on the south side of Piccadilly Circus opened in 1874 on the site of a famous coaching inn, the White Bear. It was designed in French Renaissance style by Thomas Verity, father of Frank Verity (who later extended the building), for restaurateurs Felix Spiers and Christopher Pond, with a restaurant on the first floor, ballroom above and theatre in the basement – the first theatre to be built entirely underground. The restaurant was the first place in London after the refreshment rooms at the V&A to make extensive use of decorative tiling, which Spiers and Pond had experimented with in their restaurant at Mansion House underground station, finding that it was easy to wash, while being attractive and practically indestructible. The famous Long Bar has been restored to Frank Verity's original design with gold mosaic ceiling and marble and is one of the most sumptuous accessible Victorian interiors in London. It is in the original Long Bar at the Criterion that Dr Watson first hears of Sherlock Holmes, in Arthur Conan Doyle's *A Study in Scarlet*.

Now return to the London Pavilion, turn left, cross at the lights and turn right along Shaftesbury Avenue. Opposite the red-brick and terracotta London Trocadero of 1896 turn left and take the right fork up Great Windmill Street with the Victorian St James Tavern, originally the Catherine Wheel and rebuilt in 1897, on your left. The Be At One bar on the corner of Archer street used to be the Red Lion pub, where Karl Marx and Friedrich Engels attended Communist Party meetings and put forward their proposals for the Communist Manifesto. Further up on the right is St Peter's School, which opened here in 1872 and then merged with two other charitable schools, St Anne's and St James's, to become the Soho Parish Schools. These schools, which were funded by voluntary donations, not only educated the poor children of the St Giles slums but provided medical checks and meals. Soho Parish Schools is now the only school left in Soho.

John Snow Pub

☞ CARRY ON ALONG GREAT WINDMILL STREET, THEN TURN LEFT AND RIGHT ACROSS BREWER STREET INTO LEXINGTON STREET. GO TO THE END AND ON YOUR LEFT AT THE JUNCTION WITH BROADWICK STREET IS THE VICTORIAN JOHN SNOW PUB.

This is named after the doctor who made one of the most important medical discoveries of the Victorian era by proving that cholera was a waterborne disease, rather than one carried in the air. During an outbreak of cholera in 1854, Dr Snow noticed that many of those affected by the outbreak were using water from a pump in what was then Broad Street, which was known to be heavily polluted by sewage. As an experiment he removed the handle from the pump so that it could no longer be used, and in a short time the epidemic in the area stopped. A pink kerbstone and a plaque in the pavement outside the pub on Broadwick Street mark the site of the offending pump.

☞ FROM LEXINGTON STREET TURN RIGHT INTO BROADWICK STREET AND FOLLOW IT LEFT AND RIGHT ACROSS BERWICK STREET ALL THE WAY THROUGH TO WARDOUR STREET, WHERE YOU TURN LEFT, THEN IMMEDIATELY RIGHT INTO ST ANNE'S COURT. WALK THROUGH TO DEAN STREET, TURN LEFT AND THEN RIGHT INTO CARLISLE STREET AND ON INTO SOHO SQUARE.

(22) Soho Square

Turn left to go around the square clockwise. Facing you, cunningly disguised as a Victorian office block, in black-brick and terracotta Gothic, is the French Protestant Church, the only Huguenot church left in London. It is the work of Aston Webb and was completed in 1893 as the first permanent large church for London's Protestant Huguenot community.

Continue clockwise round the square to the red-brick Italianate St Patrick's Catholic Church with its high campanile and Roman style porch with Corinthian columns. It was designed by John Kelly of Leeds and completed in 1893, the first church in England to be dedicated to St Patrick since the Reformation. It replaced the seventeenth-century Carlisle House, which had been converted into a chapel to cater for the Irish Catholics of the St Giles Rookery by an Irish Franciscan Friar, Father O'Leary, in 1791. The wonderful Italianate interior, superbly restored in 2011, is glorious.

☞ RETRACE YOUR FOOTSTEPS TO THE NORTH SIDE OF THE SQUARE, TURN RIGHT INTO SOHO STREET AND THEN LEFT INTO OXFORD STREET. CROSS THE ROAD WHEN YOU CAN, AND AT THE SECOND SET OF TRAFFIC LIGHTS TURN RIGHT INTO BERNERS STREET AND TAKE THE FIRST LEFT INTO EASTCASTLE STREET. GO PAST THE CHAMPION PUB, WHICH WAS BUILT IN 1870 AND HAD ITS VICTORIAN DECOR REFURBISHED IN THE 1920S, AND CROSS WELLS STREET.

23   Welsh Chapel
(1888)

A little further along on the right is the Welsh Chapel, or Capel Bedyddwyr Cymreig, as it says above the Corinthian colonnade guarding the entrance. Twin balustraded staircases climb up to the nave doors in front of the recessed red-brick Classical façade. The chapel was built in 1888 as a spiritual and social centre for London's rapidly growing Welsh community, and the distinctive design is the work of the Welsh architect Owen Lewis, who later became President of the Welsh Baptist Union. The interior is lovely, with a gallery on three sides supported by slim iron columns and protected by an elegant iron balustrade. One of the chief benefactors of the chapel was the

Welsh draper D.H. Evans, who set up shop in Oxford Street in 1879, and another prominent member of the congregation was David Lloyd George, whose daughter Olwen was married in the chapel in 1917.

☞ Carry on along Eastcastle Street, turn right into Great Titchfield Street and then right into Margaret Street.

(24) All Saints, Margaret Street
(1859)

On the left after 100 yards (90 m) is All Saints Church, built between 1850 and 1859 by William Butterfield and one of the most innovative and influential Victorian churches in the country, pioneer of the iconic High Victorian Gothic style that would dominate Victorian church architecture for the next 30 years. With All Saints, Butterfield did not just copy medieval Gothic but for the first time defined an authentic Victorian Gothic with its own unique features and look. All Saints is mainly of red brick with bands of black brick and stone and was the first large building in the world to use polychrome or different coloured bricks and stones in the actual structure for decoration. The effect is extraordinary and dazzling. All Saints truly is a hidden gem. Set back from this ordinary West End street behind a decorated brick arch leading into a small courtyard, the church is flanked by what, at first glance, could be two small blocks of model dwellings but these were, in fact, a choir school and vicarage. Even the spire, at 277 feet (84 m) high one of the tallest in London, is hard to spot amongst

the surrounding tall buildings. The interior of All Saints is no less magnificent, if overwhelming, with every inch of wall decorated with marble and tiles, statues and friezes, paintings and gilding. All Saints encapsulates everything we think of as Victorian in one building.

Just across the street a Buddhist temple now occupies a second parish school and church house that was built by Butterfield for All Saints in 1870.

☞ ON EXITING THE CHURCH TURN RIGHT AND GO DOWN MARGARET STREET TO REGENT STREET, WHICH IS THE THIRD CROSS STREET. TURN LEFT FOR OXFORD CIRCUS STATION AND THE END OF THE WALK.

End of walks: Oxford Circus Station

Recommended Places for Refreshment

The White Lion 24 James Street, WC2

The Nag's Head 10 James Street, WC2

The Crown 43 Monmouth Street, London, WC2

The Princess Louise 208 High Holborn, WC1

The Bloomsbury Tavern 236 Shaftesbury Avenue, WC2

The Porcupine 48 Charing Cross Road, WC2

St James Tavern 45 Great Windmill Street, W1

The John Snow 39 Broadwick Street, W1

The Champion 12–13 Wells Street, W1

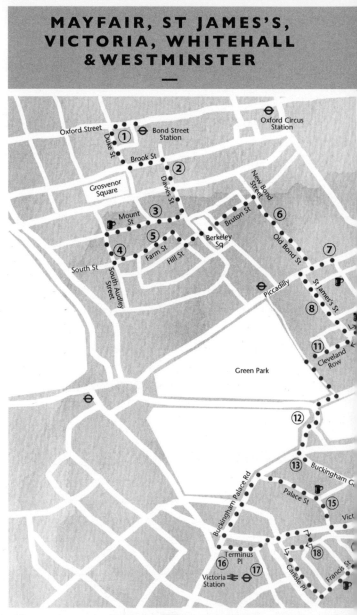

MAYFAIR, ST JAMES'S, VICTORIA, WHITEHALL & WESTMINSTER

Oxford Street

Bond Street Station

Oxford Circus Station

Duke St

Brook St

① ②

Davies St

Grosvenor Square

New Bond Street

Mount St

③

Bruton St

⑥

Berkeley Sq

Old Bond St

⑤

Farm St

Hill St

④

South St

South Audley Street

⑦

Piccadilly

St James's St

⑧

⑪

Cleveland Row

Green Park

⑫

⑬

Buckingham G

Buckingham Palace Rd

Palace St

⑮

Vict

⑯ Terminus Pl

⑱

⑰

Carlisle Pl

Francis St

Victoria Station

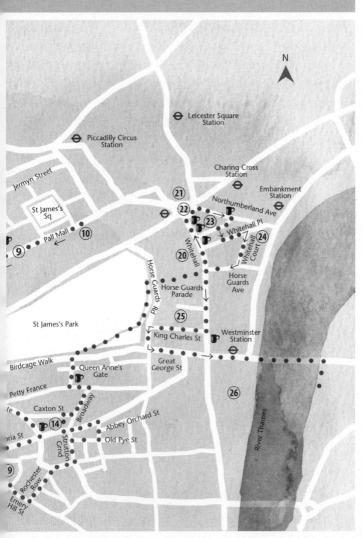

*Bond Street; Mayfair; Green Park; St James's Park;
Buckingham Palace; Horse Guards Parade; Whitehall*

N

Leicester Square
Station

Piccadilly Circus
Station

Charing Cross
Station

Jermyn Street

Embankment
Station

St James's
Sq

Northumberland Ave

㉑

㉒

㉓

Whitehall Pl

Pall Mall ⑩

㉔

⑨

Whitehall Court

㉓

⑳

Whitehall

Horse
Guards
Ave

Horse Guards Rd

Horse Guards
Parade

St James's Park

㉕

King Charles St

Westminster
Station

Birdcage Walk

Queen Anne's
Gate

Great
George St

Petty France

㉖

Caxton St

Broadway

Abbey Orchard St

⑭

ria St

Old Pye St

Struton Grnd

River Thames

⑨

Rochester Row

Emery
Hill St

231

Chapter 7

Walking in Victorian Mayfair, St James's, Victoria, Whitehall & Westminster

These walks start in Mayfair, London's most exclusive and luxurious quarter, built up through the Victorian Age by the 1st Duke of Westminster, and then take in St James's, London's clubland and playground of the rich, Royal London and finally the seat of government, Whitehall and Westminster.

Numbers applied to each attraction refer to the numbers on the map

Walks

Start walking: Bond Street Station

☞ TAKE THE W1 SHOPPING CENTRE EXIT INTO OXFORD STREET FROM THE STATION AND TURN LEFT DOWN OXFORD STREET. CROSS GILBERT STREET AND BINNEY STREET AND THEN TURN LEFT INTO DUKE STREET.

A few doors down on the left is Nelson's Homeopathic Pharmacy, founded in Ryder Street, St James's in 1860 by Ernst Armbrecht, a student of Samuel Hahnemann, the creator of homeopathy. In 1866 Armbrecht married Charlotte Nelson, who became his business partner, and he decided to change the name of the pharmacy to that of his wife. The pharmacy moved here to Duke Street in 1890. Until the 1970s, production of all Nelson's homeopathic medicines was done in the basement of the Duke Street premises. Nelson's stayed in the family for over 100 years until the remaining descendants were all killed in the Staines air disaster in 1972 and the company was taken over by Kennomeat and Kattomeat founder Dick Wilson, who had a keen interest in complementary medicine.

1 King's Weigh House Church

(1891)

Continue down Duke Street to King's Weigh House Church, now the Ukrainian Catholic Cathedral, located just off Britain's busiest shopping street but almost unknown. The church takes its unusual name from a Congregational Chapel that stood above the King's Weigh House in Eastcheap, where merchants had their goods weighed for customs duties. After several moves the church was offered a parcel of land in Mayfair by the Duke of Westminster, and the present building of red brick and cream terracotta with Romanesque arches was erected in 1891 to the design of Sir Alfred Waterhouse, architect of the Natural History Museum. The large oval auditorium has a gallery and can seat over 900 people.

Claridge's
(1856 and 1898)

☞ CONTINUE DOWN DUKE STREET ALMOST TO GROSVENOR SQUARE AND TURN LEFT INTO BROOK STREET.

After 200 yards (180 m) cross Davies Street for Claridge's Hotel, '*the first hotel in London*' according to the 1878 *Baedeker's Guide*. Butler William Claridge and his wife set up a small hotel in Brook Street in the 1840s, which was so successful that in 1855 they were able to buy the five adjoining buildings including the Minvart Hotel next door. Claridge's Hotel opened the following year in 1856. In 1860 the Empress Eugénie of France, wife of Emperor Napoleon III, stayed at Claridge's and entertained Queen Victoria and Prince Albert there, establishing the hotel's long-standing reputation as the hotel of choice for royalty. In 1893 Sir Richard D'Oyly Carte, owner of the Savoy Hotel, bought Claridge's and had the hotel rebuilt in Mayfair red brick and terracotta by C.W. Stephens, who would later go on to design Harrods. It reopened, more or less as we see it today, in 1898 and still operates the oldest working lift in London, installed during the refurbishment in 1896.

Mount Street
(1880s and 1890s)

☞ GO SOUTH ON DAVIES STREET, ALMOST TO BERKELEY SQUARE, AND TURN RIGHT INTO MOUNT STREET.

This was Mayfair's first dedicated shopping street, laid out more or less as we see it today between 1880 and 1900. It is lined with some of the best examples of the French Renaissance/ Queen Anne style red brick and pink terracotta architecture that was favoured by the 1st Duke of Westminster and very much defines his Mayfair.

No. 5, on the right (north) side, was put up in 1889 and is quite restrained, red brick and gabled with some cut and moulded ornamentation. The red brick, from the first floor upwards, was the work of Sir Ernest George and Harold Peto, son of Samuel Peto of Grissell and Peto. The Portland stone shop fronts on the ground floor were designed by different architects chosen by the shop owners.

Opposite, Nos. 125–129 was also built in 1889 and designed by W.H. Powell as shops and flats for *'persons of quality'*. It is a bit more ornate, closer perhaps to the Duke of Westminster's taste. It is certainly very pink, with beige Doulton terracotta, and has been described – by *'profane persons'*, according to *The Builder* magazine – as *'streaky bacon style'*.

Nos. 117–121, still on the south side, Flemish, with red brick and lots of pink terracotta, was built earlier, in 1886, by

James Trant Smith, and was a bit too much even for the Duke who called it *'overdone and wanting in simplicity'*. Smith was also responsible for Nos. 115 and 116 on the other side of Mount Street Mews, slightly more subdued and of a single hue, faced with pale, stone-coloured terracotta. The Victorian shop front is superb.

No. 114 is quite different, a large, rather severe terracotta block with no shops. This is because it is the Presbytery of the Jesuit Church of the Immaculate Conception on Farm Street, the back of which can be seen in Mount Street Gardens at the end of the alleyway beside the Presbytery. The Jesuit Presbytery was built in 1886–7 by Alfred Purdie, while the alleyway and gardens were laid out in 1889 to provide an approach to the Farm Street church from Mount Street.

Back on the north side, Carlos Place, which follows the curve of the road, was built in 1893 to the designs of J.E. Trollope of Giles, Gough & Trollope. It is of red brick and Portland stone and has some ornamentation as well as an interesting variety of different façades.

Across from Carlos Place is The Connaught, which began life in 1815 as the Prince of Saxe-Coburg Hotel and was completely rebuilt in 1896 by Lewis Isaacs and Henry Florence simply as the Coburg Hotel. It was renamed after Queen Victoria's son the Duke of Connaught during the Great War to allay anti-German sentiment. The somewhat controversial glass and iron shelter at the front was added in 1898. While the exterior is quite plain, red brick with stone dressings and minimal ornamentation, the inside is resplendent Victorian, with the oak-panelled dining room being particularly sumptuous.

Continuing along Mount Street, Nos, 104–113 on the south side is one range designed in two different architectural styles for different clients by the same architects, George and Peto, in 1886–7. The arched shop windows on the ground floor are of the same design along the whole range.

The long run of red-brick and terracotta shops and houses that stretches all the way along the south side to South Audley Street was built in stages between 1888 and 1895 by Albert Bolton.

The north side of this stretch of Mount Street was built between 1894 and 1898. Nos. 10–12, with the rather lovely groups of three-storey oriel windows, somewhat reminiscent of Norman Shaw, was built in 1896 by H.C. Boyes. Next the long range Nos. 113–126, ground floor of stone, red-brick upper floors with Tudor gables and mullioned windows, was built in 1898 by Herbert Read and Robert Macdonald. Note the Arts and Crafts style shop windows. On the corner with South Audley Street is the Audley Hotel, built in 1888 by the theatre designer Thomas Verity. More streaky bacon on the upper floors and flowery pink terracotta on the ground floor, but this building was apparently toned down after the Duke complained that Verity's first effort was *'too ginpalacy …'*

Directly across South Audley Street from the Audley Hotel is Audley Mansions, built in 1886 as 'first class' apartments and shops to the design of J.T. Wimperis. On the other corner is Audley House sporting a green plaque that tells us that 'James Purdey the Younger (1828–1909) Gunmaker built these premises in 1880' to house his new showrooms and workshops.

④ Thomas Goode & Co. Ltd
(1876)

Turn left into South Audley Street and go past the Grosvenor Chapel to the showrooms of Thomas Goode & Co. Ltd, purveyors of the world's finest china, silverware and glassware. This rather good red-brick building is an early work by Sir Ernest George and was erected in 1876. Note the red granite columns dividing the windows and also the variety of front gables. In the windows either side of the front entrance are the famous Thomas Goode elephants, two 7 foot (2.1 m) tall majolica elephants with ceramic howdahs and ebony. They were made by the Minton pottery company to guard the entrance to Thomas Goode & Co.'s display area at the Paris Exhibition of 1889, and they remain Minton's largest ever commission.

Turn left into South Street, noting the small windowless Italianate gallery at the side of Thomas Goode & Co. with pilasters decorated by Japanese paintings on tiled panels. Follow the road as it curves left and eventually turns into Farm Street.

⑤ Church of the Immaculate Conception
(1849)

A little way down Farm Street on the left is the Church of the Immaculate Conception, headquarters of the English Jesuits, designed by Joseph John Scoles and completed in 1849 in Decorated Gothic. The west front in Farm Street is based on the west front of Beauvais Cathedral but actually faces south because lack of space required the church to be orientated north south. The interior is superb, with red granite columns supporting the nave arcades, a wonderful nine-light 'east' window based on that of Carlisle Cathedral, Victorian mosaics in the Sanctuary and a magnificent high altar and reredos designed by Augustus Pugin, a gift from England's leading Catholic, the Duke of Norfolk. The side chapels were added in 1858 and 1878 by Henry Clutton and in 1898 by Romaine Walker.

☞ CONTINUE ALONG FARM STREET AND TURN RIGHT THEN LEFT INTO HILL STREET FOR BERKELEY SQUARE. CROSS THE ROAD AT THE PEDESTRIAN CROSSING TO YOUR RIGHT AND ENTER THE SQUARE GARDENS. GO STRAIGHT ACROSS THE GARDENS AND THEN USE THE PEDESTRIAN CROSSING TO YOUR LEFT TO CROSS THE ROAD AND GO FORWARD INTO BRUTON STREET. AFTER THE MOCK-TUDOR COACH AND HORSES TURN RIGHT INTO NEW BOND STREET.

⑥ Bond Street New and Old

Beyond the short pedestrianised stretch, note the glorious early Victorian shop front of Asprey's, with huge windows divided by slim iron columns installed in 1848 when Asprey's moved into the property. A plaque on the wall of the building facing Grafton Street informs us that the great Victorian actor Henry Irving lived here from 1872 until 1899 – one thing I hadn't realised about him is that he was the first person to suggest dimming the lights in the auditorium so as to focus attention on the stage.

Continue down New Bond Street, which turns into Old Bond Street at Burlington Gardens. Tiffany & Co at No. 25 on the right has a fine Victorian shop-front, designed in 1865 by F.P. Cockerell, the windows a little smaller and the columns a little thicker than those of Asprey's. The Arcade at No. 28 linking Old Bond Street with Albemarle Street, was built in 1879 and is the best preserved Victorian shopping arcade in London, with its beautifully curved glass window bays, elaborate stuccoed façade and its glass roof. Queen Victoria visited in the 1880s to buy a shirt from H.W. Bretall and gave the Arcade its Royal prefix, while the Prince of Wales, later Edward VII, was partial to a Charbonnel et Walker chocolate from the chocolate emporium established in the Arcade by Madamoiselle Charbonnel in 1874. Apparently, Henry Irving's leading actress Ellen Terry was a devotee as well.

No. 31 (Nirav Modi), on the right, is by Arthur Beresford Pite, known for his work on the Institute of Chartered Accountants headquarters off Moorgate, and was built in 1898. Note Pite's trademark, the two statues of crouching women above the door. The red-brick and terracotta No. 43 was designed in 1877 by Edward Salomons, architect of the New West End Synagogue in Bayswater. No. 1A, Mappin and Webb, on the corner with Piccadilly, red brick and cream terracotta, is by the great Sir Alfred Waterhouse and was built in 1880.

⑦ Burlington House
(1873)

Turn left into Piccadilly and walk past the Burlington Arcade to Burlington House. The original Burlington House was built around 1665 and was remodelled for the

1st Earl of Burlington as one of the first Palladian buildings in England. In 1854 the government bought the house and in 1857 three learned societies, the Royal Society, the Linnean Society (the world's oldest biological society) and the Royal Society of Chemistry, moved in. In 1867 the Royal Academy of Arts joined them. In 1872 Sydney Smirke added a third storey to the original house to provide additional space for the Royal Academy and added exhibition halls in the gardens behind the main house. Further work was done by Norman Shaw in 1883. Meanwhile, in 1873, architects Robert Banks and Edward Barry had been brought in to extend the house for the use of the three learned societies and by the end of 1873 they had built the grand Italianate range facing Piccadilly and the two slightly less palatial east and west wings enclosing the courtyard. The three learned societies moved in there in 1873. In 1874 they were joined by the Geological Society (the world's first geological society), the Royal Astronomical Society and the Society of Antiquaries. The Royal Society moved out to Carlton Terrace in 1968 but the other five societies are still there.

In 1858 Charles Darwin and Alfred Russel Wallace presented a joint paper on the 'Theory of Evolution' to the Linnean Society in a room in the main house, now called the Reynolds Room.

⑧ St James's Street

 ☞ ON LEAVING BURLINGTON HOUSE TURN RIGHT, CROSS PICCADILLY AT THE LIGHTS, THEN GO RIGHT AND LEFT INTO ST JAMES'S STREET.

First on the right (west), the Classical Portland stone building with the huge Corinthian columns was built for Crockford's gambling club in 1827. Crockford's closed in 1844 and between 1870 and 1875 the building was restyled as we see it now by theatre architect C.J. Phipps for the Devonshire Club, a Liberal gentleman's club established in 1874 as an alternative to the Liberal Reform Club. No. 63, also on the west side, is Portland stone with Baroque embellishments and has been variously described as 'tasteless' (Pevsner) or 'vulgar' (London survey). It is certainly unashamedly Victorian and was designed in 1888 by Davis and Emmanuel for the Meistersingers' Club and later, in 1894, the Royal Societies Club. No. 68 stands out as the only red brick on the west side. It has a fine Victorian shop front with cast-iron columns and was built in 1901 by Charles Mileham for the locksmiths Chubb & Son, who stayed there until 1975. William Evans the gunmakers, who now occupy the premises, were established in 1883.

If you are looking for refreshment at this point, go a few yards along King Street, on the left, to the Victorian Golden Lion pub, all dark wood and stained glass, where Oscar Wilde and actress Lillie Langtry would relax after a performance at the St James's Theatre, which stood opposite in Victorian times. A little further along, in Duke of York Street, to the north of St James's Square, is the Red Lion pub. This has Corinthian pilasters outside and mahogany frames and frosted glass panels inside, and was described in the *Architectural Review* as a *'perfect example … of the small Victorian Gin Palace at its best'*. Next door is G.E. Trumper the gentleman's barbers, established in nearby Curzon Street in 1875 by George Trumper.

Back in St James's Street, No. 9 is the bespoke workshop of John Lobb the boot-maker, established here in 1866 and boot-maker to Queen Victoria and also to the Prince of Wales, later Edward VII.

Further down on the west side, No. 78, huge, Portland stone, Palladian, was built in 1845 by Sydney Smirke for the Conservative Club, set up in 1840 for rebellious Conservatives who had upset the Conservative Carlton Club up the road at No. 69. The Conservative Club moved out in 1959 and the building is now occupied by a bank.

Next door, No. 86 is unmistakably Victorian, heavy Italianate and reminiscent of the Grosvenor Hotel at Victoria Station, which is unsurprising as it was designed by the same architect, James Knowles Jr. The carved foliage ornamentation climbing up the façade is the work of John Daymond, who also worked on the Grosvenor Hotel. No. 86 was built in 1862 and first occupied by the Civil Service Club from 1866 to 1869. In 1870 it became home to the Thatched House Club, established in 1865 for gentlemen with no political affiliation and named after the celebrated Thatched House Tavern, which had originally stood on the site. It is now the Mark Masons' Hall.

Across the road on the corner of St James's Street and Pall Mall the red-brick building with stone bands was designed by Norman Shaw in his inimitable style in 1882.

9 Pall Mall

Now turn left for a quick detour along Pall Mall to see Sir Charles Barry's masterpiece, the Reform Club.

No. 71, on the south side, quietly Classical with four columns guarding the entrance is the Oxford and Cambridge Club, designed by Sir Robert and Sydney Smirke and opened in 1838. Nos. 77–78 was designed by Thomas Wyatt in 1862–3 and lived in by Queen Victoria's daughter Princess Christian. The building is now offices. No. 79 was designed in Italianate style by Wyatt's partner David Brandon for the Eagle Star Insurance Company in 1868. No. 22, on the north side, is in Norman Shaw's Queen Anne style and is the only red-brick intrusion on Pall Mall. It was built in 1880 to the design of R.F. Russell.

⑩ Reform Club
(1841)

Finally, on the south side stands the great Portland stone mass of the Reform Club. The club was founded in 1836 by Edward Ellice of the Hudson's Bay Company, a champion of the Reform Act of 1832, and was intended as a club for those of a liberal and progressive persuasion. The clubhouse was designed by Sir Charles Barry, built by Grissell and Peto and opened in 1841. The design is based on the Palazzo Farnese in Rome and was an advance on the smaller Traveller's Club of 1832 next door, also by Barry, which was itself ground-breaking, being the first entirely Italian Renaissance style building in England, and the first large Victorian building to be designed without columns. The Reform Club's saloon is considered to be the finest clubroom in London. Originally intended as a courtyard, it is covered by a huge coved cast-iron roof and consists of two storeys with colonnades of yellow scagliola, portraits in niches

along the red walls and coloured marbles by Edward Barry. The Reform Club's chef was the first celebrity chef, Alexis Soyer, who helped Barry design the kitchens and introduced numerous innovations, such as cooking with gas, ovens with adjustable temperatures and refrigerators cooled by water. His trademark dish, Lamb Cutlet Reform, is still on the menu today. Isambard Kingdom Brunel, William Makepeace Thackeray, Viscount Palmerston and William Gladstone were amongst the members, as was Richard Cobden, who championed the Repeal of the Corn Laws in 1846. True to its radical beginnings the Reform Club was the first of London's gentlemen's clubs to admit women as members, in 1981. It was in the smoking room of the Reform Club that Phineas Fogg, the Jules Verne character who went around the world in 80 days, agreed to accept the challenge from his fellow members, and from the steps of the club that he set off.

Bridgewater House
(1854)

☞ Now return along Pall Mall to St James's Palace and go straight ahead into Cleveland Row. Bear right at the end.

Here is one of London's most beautiful Victorian houses, Bridgewater House, built for Lord Ellesmere, heir to the canal builder the 3rd Duke of Bridgewater. It is a refreshingly unfussy palazzo by Sir Charles Barry, much smaller and simpler than his Reform Club. Barry also designed many of the chimney-pieces, doors and ceilings. The house was completed in 1854, although the purpose-built art gallery inside the house, where the Bridgewater and Sutherland art collections were on display to the public, opened in 1851. Bridgewater House now belongs to the Latsis shipping family.

☞ Walk through the passageway between Bridgewater House and Selwyn House into Green Park and bear left for Buckingham Palace.

Buckingham Palace
(1847)

The iconic east front of Buckingham Palace, facing the Mall and known to millions across the world, was designed by Edward Blore and built by Thomas Cubitt in 1847, and was later slightly remodelled in 1913. In 1761 George III bought what was then the townhouse of the Duke of Buckingham as a home for his wife Queen Charlotte. George IV asked John Nash to transform the house into a palace, and so Nash added

two wings to make a three-sided courtyard and placed the
Marble Arch on the open east side to form a grand entrance.
George IV died before he could move in and William IV
commissioned Edward Blore to finish the work. William hated
the place and never moved in but his niece Victoria, when she
became Queen in 1837, leapt at the chance to leave the stifling
confines of Kensington Palace and moved in two weeks after her
accession to the throne, thus becoming the first monarch to live
in Buckingham Palace. In 1840 Victoria married Prince Albert
and the palace soon became too small for the growing Royal
Family and the expanding Royal Court, so Edward Blore was
brought in to add more rooms. He moved the Marble Arch to its
present site at the top of Park Lane and enclosed the courtyard
with the east front, complete with the famous balcony from

where the monarch could wave to the crowds on state occasions. The balcony was first used specifically for such a purpose in 1851, when Queen Victoria greeted the crowds celebrating the opening of the Great Exhibition, and then again in 1853, when the Queen watched the Scots and Coldstream Guards parade before marching off to the Crimean War.

Buckingham Gate

☞ AS YOU FACE THE PALACE, TURN LEFT AND, KEEPING THE PALACE TO YOUR RIGHT, WALK ALONG SPUR ROAD, GO TO THE SECOND SET OF LIGHTS AND CROSS BUCKINGHAM GATE TO THE STUCCO PALAZZO AT No. 10 ON THE CORNER.

This was built in 1854 as offices for the Duchy of Cornwall by Sir James Pennethorne, nephew of John Nash, architect of the original Buckingham Palace. The Duchy still resides there. Note the Prince of Wales feathers on the railings. As you stand outside No. 10 turn around and look back at Buckingham Palace across the road. The large building of golden stone in the distance to the left, with the pedimented windows, which rises above the grey stone three-storey building with the black roof, is the Buckingham Palace ballroom, added in 1856 by the same Sir James Pennethorne. At 123 feet (37 m) long and 60 feet (18 m) wide, it was the largest room in London at the time it was built. The first ball to be held in the new ballroom took place that same year to celebrate the end of the Crimean War.

☞ AS YOU FACE No. 10, TURN LEFT DOWN BUCKINGHAM GATE.

No. 20, a little way down on the right, is very attractive in red brick with stone bands and was built in 1895 for the banker Emil Heinemann by Reginald Blomfield, nephew of Sir Arthur Blomfield, architect of the Royal College of Music in South Kensington. Note the oriel window, unusual stepped gable and frieze above the fourth-floor windows.

Further down on the right is Westminster Chapel Evangelical Free Church. It is built in yellow brick, with stone and red-brick dressings, in what the *Illustrated London News* called 'Lombardic' Romanesque style and was completed in 1865 by William Poulton. The oval interior holds 1,500 people and is enormous, with two galleries and a wide, open-span roof. This chapel replaces a previous Congregational chapel of 1841, which became too small. The chapel can be appreciated in its full glory from Petty France, opposite.

A little further along Buckingham Gate are the red-brick and stone dressings of St James's Court, eight blocks of service apartments built above the Circle Line between 1896 and 1899 by J. Chirney Pawley. The apartments are gathered around an open courtyard, which is decorated with green tiles, a long terracotta figure frieze illustrating stories from Shakespeare and a contemporary cast-iron fountain. Each individual staircase is guarded by caryatids, columns fashioned in the shape of a female figure.

The Albert
(1862)

Buckingham Gate now curves round to the right to meet Victoria Street, cut through a former slum area known as Devil's Acre in the 1850s and 1860s. On the corner is the Albert pub, built in 1862 by Joseph Wood, the owner of the Artillery Brewery, and the only building left from the initial development of the street. It is built of yellow brick with red-brick dressings and is capped with a huge stucco parapet around the roofline. The Albert also survived the Blitz and is

perhaps the best preserved complete Victorian pub in London, both inside and out, retaining many original features, such as the ornate ceilings, hand-etched frosted glass windows and wrought-iron balconies.

☞ TURN RIGHT ON TO VICTORIA STREET AND FIRST RIGHT INTO PALACE STREET, SITE IN 1860 OF WATNEY'S BREWERY.

On the right, tucked away behind some modern school buildings, is the Gothic main building of Westminster City School, built in 1876 by R.R. Arntz, with a bronze of philanthropist Sir Sydney Waterlow in the courtyard.

St Peter and St Edward
Catholic Church
(1863)

Beyond the school on either side of Castle Lane are two blocks of workmen's dwellings built by Watney's in the 1860s, followed by the Presbytery of St Peter and St Edward Roman Catholic church, yellow brick with red-brick dressings and Queen Anne overtones, built in 1880 by J.F. Bentley, architect of Westminster Cathedral. The church itself is located on Wilfred Street and was built in 1863 by William Wardell above a mission chapel of 1856. The high altar and south altar were made by Bentley in neo-Gothic fashion in the 1860s, and there is an unusual font by Doulton.

Grosvenor Hotel
(1861)

☞ CONTINUE TO THE END OF PALACE STREET, PAST
THE QUEEN'S LOCAL, THE VICTORIAN CASK AND GLASS,
SAID TO BE THE SMALLEST PUB IN CENTRAL LONDON,
TURN LEFT INTO BUCKINGHAM PALACE ROAD AND WALK
FOR FIVE MINUTES TO VICTORIA STATION.

The station is dominated by the enormous Paris Italianate style Grosvenor Hotel of 1861, built in what was once honey-coloured Bath stone by James Knowles and James Knowles Jr, father and son. The Parisian overtones come from the pavilion roofs, amongst the first seen in London. The Grosvenor was one of London's grandest nineteenth-century hotels and the first in the world to install *'ascending rooms'* or lifts, powered by water pressure. There was also a bathroom on every floor, except the top floor, which was for servants. The lobby is still a most impressive place to take tea. Note the medallions on the first and top floors, which contain carved busts of Queen Victoria and Prince Albert and some early Victorian Prime Ministers, including Lord Russell, the Earl of Derby and Viscount Palmerston.

(17) Victoria Station
(1860)

Victoria Station is two stations in one. In 1860 the London, Brighton and South Coast Railway opened their new terminus at the end of the just finished Victoria Street, the tracks carried over the river on the newly built Grosvenor Railway Bridge, the first railway bridge across the Thames in central London. This was constructed by Sir John Fowler, engineer of the Metropolitan Railway, who later built the train sheds for the London, Chatham and Dover Railway's new Westminster terminus, which opened alongside the London Brighton station to the east in 1862. In 1865 the Grosvenor Bridge was widened to improve service to both stations. The stations had different entrances and remained completely separate until 1924, when Southern Railway took over both of them and knocked through the dividing wall. The Grosvenor Hotel, first of the great railway hotels, is the only building from the original station complex that survives more or less intact, the other buildings at the station front having been remodelled in the first decade of the 1900s.

☞ KEEP TO THE LEFT AS YOU WALK THROUGH THE BUS STATION, WITH THE RAILWAY STATIONS ON YOUR RIGHT, AND BEAR LEFT AROUND VICTORIA BUILDINGS, WHICH WERE CONSTRUCTED ABOVE VICTORIA UNDERGROUND STATION IN 1872. CROSS THE ROAD TO YOUR RIGHT AT THE LIGHTS. ON THE CENTRAL ISLAND IS LITTLE BEN, A MINIATURE VERSION OF BIG BEN, FIRST ERECTED HERE IN 1892. GO STRAIGHT AHEAD PAST LITTLE BEN, CROSS AT THE LIGHTS INTO VICTORIA STREET AND WALK ALONG TO WESTMINSTER CATHEDRAL ON YOUR RIGHT.

(18) Westminster Cathedral
(1895)

Seat of the Archbishop of Westminster and Mother Church of the Roman Catholic Church of England and Wales, the Metropolitan Cathedral of the Most Precious Blood was begun in 1895 and opened in 1903. Not wanting his cathedral to upstage or be upstaged by the Gothic masterpiece of Westminster Abbey at the other end of Victoria Street, Cardinal Vaughan asked his architect J.F. Bentley to come up with something in an earlier Christian style, hence the sensational Byzantine appearance. The cathedral is built entirely of red brick with proportional bands of Portland stone and with no steel reinforcement. Sir John Betjeman commented that the cathedral looks bigger on the inside than the outside and this is true. The nave is the widest in England, 156 feet (48 m) across and flanked with chapels ablaze with mosaics. The whole interior is eventually to be covered in mosaics and marble, but due to expense this work is still in

progress, so the upper walls of the nave and the ceiling have been left as dark brick, which creates a spectacular effect with the high domes disappearing into inky blackness. The church is decorated with 126 different kinds of marble, from all over the world, the greatest variety of marble in any building in Britain.

For a peaceful and unhurried bird's-eye view of the Victorian London you are discovering on this walk, take the lift to the Viewing Gallery, located near the top of the 273 foot (83 m) high Italianate campanile, one of London's least known viewpoints.

⑲ Victoria Conservation Area

☞ ON EXITING THE CATHEDRAL TURN IMMEDIATELY LEFT
AND WALK ALONG ASHLEY PLACE TO CARLISLE PLACE.

The next leg of the walk goes through an area of Victorian townscape that is almost untouched, a world of mansion blocks, social housing, ecclesiastical buildings and charitable foundations. Evelyn Mansions, across the road, was built in 1893. Turn left into Carlisle Place. Nos, 1–3, a little way down on the left, with yellow-brick façade and simple Italianate details, was built in 1860 by W. Jackson and designed by Charles Parnell as one of London's earliest mansion blocks and it is now the oldest surviving mansion block in London. Opposite, the Venetian palazzo of St Vincent's Centre, its Italianate details picked out in fresh new pink and white paintwork, was built as a girl's orphanage for the Daughters of Charity by Henry Clutton in 1862, with additions in 1878. Further along is Carlisle Mansions, lining both sides of the road but slightly different on either side. These blocks were built in 1886, as it says on the central Dutch gable of the mansions on the right-hand side, while Cardinal Mansions, on the left at the end, was built in 1898 by George Baines. The Manning House palazzo opposite is of 1865 and was designed by the Peabody architect Henry Darbishire. It served as the Archbishop of Westminster's Palace from 1873 to 1901 and is now offices.

Turn left into Francis Street. The yellow-brick building with the monastic style arcade was designed as a Franciscan friary by Henry Darbishire in 1865. Note the statue of Saint Francis at first-floor level on the corner. Opposite is Morpeth Mansions of 1891. Further on, take a look up Ambrosden Avenue on the left. The Archbishop's House and Diocesan Hall on the left are all part of the Westminster Cathedral complex built between 1895 and 1902 and designed by Bentley. The warehouse-like building of dark red brick on the right at No. 1 Ambrosden Avenue is United House, a former Police Section House, built in 1890. Further up Ambrosden Avenue, on the right, you can see the striped white stone and red brick of a block of the huge, luxurious Ashley Gardens estate, built in stages between 1883 and 1893 and covering several blocks of the surrounding streets.

Back in Francis Street, the tall, yellow-brick block on the right is Coburg Buildings, built in 1875 by Sir Sydney Waterlow's Improved Industrial Dwellings Corporation. If you go round into narrow Windsor Place and look up, there is a plaque set high on the wall explaining exactly that. Note the fine Victorian wrought-iron railings running around the building. Next door is the Windsor Castle pub, formerly The Cardinal. It was built around 1880 and has a splendid timber and granite Victorian pub front.

☞ TURN RIGHT INTO EMERY HILL STREET. GO TO THE END AND TURN LEFT INTO ROCHESTER ROW.

St Stephen's Church, a very typical fourteenth-century Gothic style Victorian church with a tall spire, was designed by Benjamin Ferry. Completed in 1847, it was built for Baroness Burdett-Coutts as a memorial to her father. The Tennant Chapel inside, dedicated to Baroness Burdett-Coutts's god-daughter Angela Tennant, has some fine mosaics and there is stained glass by Edward Burne-Jones. Behind the church, down Rochester Street, is the Burdett-Coutts and Townshend School built in 1849, also by Ferry, and paid for by the Baroness. The rather fine red-brick building across the road from the church, with the square cupola and Dutch gables, is the main block of the United Westminster Almshouses, built in 1882 and designed by R.R. Arnteg. At the end of each wing there is a bust of the two seventeenth-century philanthropists, the Reverend James Palmer and Emery Hill, who founded the original almshouses, which were united here in 1879.

☞ NOW CONTINUE ALONG ROCHESTER ROW AND BEAR RIGHT AT THE ROUNDABOUT INTO GREYCOAT PLACE, THEN LEFT AT THE NEXT ROUNDABOUT INTO COBBLED STRUTTON GROUND.

Strutton Ground was the home of a thriving market in Victorian times, with 119 costers recorded selling their wares here in 1865. The market still operates on weekdays, although on a somewhat smaller scale.

☞ ALMOST AT THE END OF STRUTTON GROUND TURN RIGHT INTO OLD PYE STREET.

A little way down on the right is Rochester Buildings, put up in 1862 and paid for by the philanthropist William Gibbs. The block was designed by the Peabody architect Henry Darbishire and later sold to Peabody in 1877. Further along is the vast Abbey Orchard Street estate, put up by Peabody in the 1870s and built, again by Henry Darbishire, to the traditional Peabody design in two-tone yellow brick.

☞ TURN LEFT UP ABBEY ORCHARD STREET AND TURN LEFT ON TO VICTORIA STREET. GO ACROSS STRUTTON GROUND AND IMMEDIATELY CROSS VICTORIA STREET USING THE LIGHTS ON YOUR RIGHT. HAVING CROSSED THE ROAD TURN LEFT AND WALK ALONG TO THE END OF THE SMALL PATCH OF GREEN.

Immediately across the road is the tall Gothic arched entrance to Artillery Mansions, built in 1895 by John Calder. Turn right and walk along the alleyway beside the green to Caxton Street. In front of you is Caxton Hall, designed in elaborate French Renaissance style by William Lee and F.J. Smith and opened as Westminster City Hall in 1882. Caxton Hall became famous for suffragette rallies and fashionable weddings, but the main body of the building has been completely rebuilt and just the front section of the Victorian building survives.

☞ TURN RIGHT ALONG CAXTON STREET, LEFT ALONG BROADWAY, LEFT INTO PETTY FRANCE AND RIGHT AT THE ROUNDABOUT INTO QUEEN ANNE'S GATE.

No. 29 Queen Anne's Gate on the right, with red brick, white-painted brick bands, Dutch gables and a heavy pediment over the door, was built in 1888 as flats and is now offices. Go straight on down the narrow passageway, past the gates and across Birdcage Walk into St James's Park. Bear right towards Horse Guards Parade, keeping the lake on your left. When you reach Horse Guards Road bear left along the path inside the park around the lake. On your left is a small Swiss-looking cottage orne – a picturesque style building – which was erected in 1840 for the Royal Ornithological Society to house a Bird Keeper, whose job it was to watch over the park's valuable bird and wildfowl collection. The cottage, which was designed by John Burges Watson, sits on Duck Island and is connected to what was the Society's clubhouse by a loggia style bridge. Today it is home to the London Historic Parks and Gardens Trust, who look after the lodge garden and sometimes put on exhibitions inside the cottage.

Continue through the park to the Guards Memorial and then walk across Horse Guards Parade, where the funeral procession for the Duke of Wellington gathered in 1852. The Queen Anne style red-brick and stone building on your left, with the copper domes, is part of the Old Admiralty and was built in 1898–1902. Go through the arch into Whitehall.

⑳ Whitehall

Cross Whitehall at the lights. Ahead of you is the Baroque Old War Office, designed by William Young in 1898 and completed by his son in 1907.

☞ TURN LEFT IN FRONT OF THE WAR OFFICE AND PROCEED ALONG WHITEHALL TOWARDS TRAFALGAR SQUARE.

The Clarence pub at the corner with Great Scotland Yard dates from 1892. The Old Shades a bit further along, with a half-timbered oak pub front and a rather fancy gable that looks as though it has been bolted on, was built in 1898 by Treadwell & Martin, who also designed the next-door Whitehall House in 1907. Two doors on is the Silver Cross Tavern, which originally occupied just the red-brick house. It was first licensed in 1674 and has been rebuilt many times, the last time being in 1900, and it has a splendid Victorian interior of tiles, mirrors and marble.

㉑ Trafalgar Square

Now cross over into Trafalgar Square. The square was begun by John Nash, who began clearing the area in 1826, but most of it was built in the early Victorian era to the design of Sir

Charles Barry. The first structure to be built was the National Gallery on the north side, which was intended to be the defining backdrop to the square but rather disappoints in its lack of grandeur, although this is partly explained by the lack of space, which allowed for the building to be just one room deep. The gallery was designed by William Wilkins and completed in 1838, with additions by Sir James Pennethorne in 1861. Edward Barry remodelled the galleries inside as we see them today between 1872 and 1876. The square itself was initially built on a slope, and in 1840 Sir Charles Barry corrected this by constructing the northern terrace in front of the National Gallery with steps leading down to the main square.

Nelson's Column
1843

The celebrated monument to Lord Nelson, a 145 foot (44 m) high fluted Corinthian column made of Devon granite, was designed by Clapham-born architect William Railton, and raised in 1843. The statue of Nelson that stands on top is 17 feet (5 m) tall and is made of Craigleith granite from Scotland. It was sculpted by E.H. Baily. The statue stands on a bronze base made from guns from the Woolwich Arsenal foundry. The bronze bas-relief panels at the base of the column show scenes from Nelson's battles and were completed in 1849. The four lions were sculpted by the animal painter Sir Edwin Landseer and although they were part of the original design they were not unveiled until 1868, a quarter of a century after the column went up, their non-appearance becoming something of a national joke. Landseer modelled the lions on a real lion from London Zoo that had died and been installed in his studio, but he was not confident of his ability to complete the project and took so long to make his sketches that the lion decomposed. As a result the lion's paws look more like cat's paws, while in real life the back of a reposing lion is convex rather than concave as on Landseer's lions. They are, nonetheless, magnificent beasts.

Sir Charles Barry apparently disapproved of having Nelson's Column in the square as he wanted to keep it clear of monuments. Nevertheless he agreed to design a pair of fountains, which were added in 1845, to restrict the amount of public gathering space. These were replaced by larger fountains after the Second World War and the originals were sent to Canada, where one can be seen in Ottawa's Confederation Park and the other in a park in Regina, capital of Saskatchewan.

Set into the wall of the northern terrace, behind the café benches near the eastern set of steps, are the Standard Imperial Measures, placed here in 1876 so that people could come and check the accuracy of their measuring instruments.

☞ NOW LEAVE TRAFALGAR SQUARE THE WAY YOU CAME, BUT INSTEAD OF GOING BACK DOWN WHITEHALL GO INTO NORTHUMBERLAND AVENUE.

This short street was laid out in 1876 to link Charing Cross with the Embankment and was originally full of vast hotels, such as the seven-storey arcaded building on the left, which opened as the Grand Hotel in 1880. Further along on the right, No. 8 was the Victoria Hotel, designed by L.H. Isaacs and H.L. Florence in a quietly elegant French Renaissance style and opened in 1887. Further still, beyond Great Scotland Yard, is the Corinthia Hotel, opened as the Metropole Hotel in 1885 and designed by F. & H. Francis and J.E. Saunders. Opposite Great Scotland Yard, in Northumberland Street, is the Sherlock Holmes pub, a Victorian themed pub that occupies what was originally the Northumberland Hotel, built in 1880 – probably the hotel that appears by that name in the Sherlock Holmes novel *The Hound of the Baskervilles*. Next door, at No. 25 Northumberland Avenue, are the Turkish baths frequented by Holmes and Watson in *The Adventure of the Noble Batchelor*.

☞ NOW TURN INTO GREAT SCOTLAND YARD.

Scotland Yard

Nigeria House, on the corner, was built in Italianate style in 1879 by John Gibson, of Gibson Hall, Bishopsgate (*See* pages 105–06), and was extended along Great Scotland Yard by Sir Alfred Waterhouse in the 1890s. Turn the corner and there, looking completely out of place amongst all the Baroque splendour of Whitehall, is the wonderfully spooky Old Fire House, built in 1884 in Frenchified style and dark red brick. It served as a fire station until 1922 and is now the home of the Civil Service Club.

☞ TURN LEFT INTO SCOTLAND PLACE AND GO UNDER THE BRIDGE INTO WHITEHALL PLACE.

This road was created out of Middle and Little Scotland Yard, site of the lodgings of the Kings of Scotland when they came to stay at Whitehall Palace. In 1829 Sir Robert Peel used No. 4 Whitehall Place as the first headquarters for his newly formed Metropolitan Police. There was an entrance at the rear of the building on to Great Scotland Yard, and this, the world's first official police station, became known as Scotland Yard. In 1890 the Metropolitan Police moved to New Scotland Yard, a larger, purpose-built headquarters designed by Norman Shaw at the other end of Whitehall.

National Liberal Club
(1887)

Turn left down Whitehall Place and on the right-hand side at the end is the National Liberal Club, founded in 1882 by Liberal Prime Minister William Gladstone as an alternative to the exclusive Reform Club. This was a place where ordinary Liberal party members could meet and debate – and members are still required to refrain from anti-liberal political activities. Designed by Sir Alfred Waterhouse in a French château style so as to blend in with the adjoining Whitehall Court, the club opened in 1887. With numerous club rooms, dining rooms and over 140 bedrooms, it was the largest clubhouse ever built, and remained so until overtaken by the RAC Club in Pall Mall in 1910, and was the first building in London to have an electrically powered lift and to be lit throughout by electricity. It was also one of the first buildings in the world, if not *the* first, to make use of a steel frame. The club wine cellar was fashioned out of a trench excavated in 1865 for the proposed Waterloo to Whitehall underground railway that was later abandoned. The interior is liberally decorated with Waterhouses's beloved glazed and patterned tiles, so much so that F.E. Smith, later Lord Birkenhead, although not a member, would drop in to use the ornate facilities on his way to Parliament. When challenged he declared, '*Good heavens, I had no idea this was a club as well as a lavatory!*'

Turn right in front of the National Liberal Club and walk down Whitehall Court. The building called Whitehall Court was built as apartments by Archer & Green in 1884 and is now occupied by the Farmers Club, as well as apartments, offices and the Royal Horse Guards Hotel, which took over many of the National Liberal Club's bedrooms. The turrets and pinnacles of Whitehall Court form a good part of the famous view from the bridge spanning the lake in St James's Park.

Foreign and Commonwealth Office
(1873)

☞ GO TO THE END OF WHITEHALL COURT, TURN RIGHT INTO HORSE GUARDS AVENUE, CROSS WHITEHALL AND TURN LEFT.

Just past the entrance to Downing Street on your right is the Foreign and Commonwealth Office. Turn right down King Charles Street for the main entrance. It was built between 1868 and 1873 and designed by Sir George Gilbert Scott as *'a kind of national palace, or drawing-room for the nation'*. Scott's first design was for a Gothic building, but this was rejected by the Prime Minister, Lord Palmerston, who wanted a Classical building for the first purpose-built home for the Foreign Office. Scott reluctantly obliged, but did allow himself a little hint of Gothic on the west front overlooking St James's Park. The building was originally designed to house four Government Offices, the Foreign Office, the India Office, the Colonial Office and the Home Office, one on each corner around an individual courtyard and all sharing a central courtyard. The stately rooms inside were designed by Scott to impress foreign visitors and reflect Britain's influence in the world, and they are sumptuous. The grandest are the three rooms that make up the Locarno Suite: the Cabinet Room, with its barrel-vaulted roof, the Dining Room and the Conference Room with a gilded ceiling, all of them originally decorated by Clayton & Bell and restored in the late 1980s. Another highlight is the marble Grand Staircase, which divides as it rises through three floors beneath a gilded dome, past arcaded galleries decorated by Clayton & Bell and mosaic floors by Minton. At the heart of the India Office is the Durbar Court, the work of Matthew Digby Wyatt. It was originally open to the sky but was covered over by an iron and glass roof in 1868, has a marble floor and is surrounded by three storeys of arches with granite columns and a mass of statuary. All these marvellous Victorian interiors can be seen during Open London Weekend.

☞ GO DOWN THE STEPS AT THE END OF KING CHARLES STREET INTO HORSE GUARDS ROAD TO SEE THE FULL EXTENT OF THE FOREIGN OFFICE BUILDING. TURN LEFT, GO PAST THE TREASURY BUILDING ON THE LEFT AND TURN LEFT INTO GREAT GEORGE STREET FOR PARLIAMENT SQUARE AND THE HOUSES OF PARLIAMENT. FOR THE BEST VIEW GO ON THROUGH PARLIAMENT SQUARE, LAID OUT IN 1868 BY SIR CHARLES BARRY TO PROVIDE A DIGNIFIED APPROACH TO THE HOUSES OF PARLIAMENT, STRAIGHT INTO BRIDGE STREET AND OVER WESTMINSTER BRIDGE, BUILT IN 1862 AND PAINTED GREEN TO MATCH THE BENCHES IN THE HOUSE OF COMMONS, THEN RIGHT ON TO THE EMBANKMENT.

(26) Houses of Parliament
(1840–70)

Seen from across the River Thames, the Houses of Parliament, or the Palace of Westminster, is probably the most recognisable Parliament building in the world. It replaced the old Palace of Westminster – originally the reigning monarch's main residence and then the home of Parliament – which burned down in 1834, at the twilight of the Georgian/Regency period. The laying of the new building's foundation stone in 1840 marked the dawn of the Victorian Age. The magnificent home of the Mother of Parliaments is not only a London icon but a symbol of Victorian power and belief, as well as of modern democracy. The brief for the new building was for one in the English style, which meant Elizabethan or Gothic, and the architect, Sir Charles Barry, chose fifteenth-century Perpendicular Gothic, even though he was more of a Classical man, as shown by his Reform Club (*see* page 245). To help, he chose the leading Gothic architect of the time, Augustus Pugin, and the Houses of Parliament we see today, which took 30 years to complete, are very much the work of the two of them, although Pugin concentrated more on the interior.

The Palace covers 8 acres (3.2 ha), has 11 courtyards, 100 staircases, nearly 3 miles (5 km) of passageway and over 1,100 rooms, and the river frontage is 940 feet (287 m) long. At the southern end of the building is the Victoria Tower, named after the Queen and designed to resemble a castle keep. At 323 feet (98 m) high, it was the tallest secular building in the world at the time of its completion and holds the Parliamentary Archives, consisting of over 3 million records dating back to 1497 and stored on over 5 miles (8 km) of shelving.

The central spire is 300 feet (91 m) tall and rises above the Central Lobby, midway between the Lords Chamber (completed in 1847) and the Commons Chamber (completed in 1852).

At the northern end stands the Clock Tower, 316 feet (96 m) high and renamed the Elizabeth Tower in 2012 to mark the Diamond Jubilee of Elizabeth II. This tower, which was designed by Augustus Pugin, is home to the world's most famous clock, the Great Clock, commonly known as Big Ben, although in reality this is the name of the clock's hour bell, which takes its name either from Sir Benjamin Hall, the Chief Commissioner of Works, or Benjamin Caunt, a popular prize fighter of the time, whose nickname was Big Ben. The Great Clock's reputation for reliability stems from the requirements of the Astronomer Royal, George Airy, who demanded that the first stroke of the hour bell should register the hour correct to within one second and telegraph it twice a day to the Royal Observatory at Greenwich. Such accuracy was considered impossible, but the Great Clock, which was built by Edward Dent, has remained consistently accurate to within one second since it first rang out across London on 31 May 1859. The clock's accuracy is regulated by adding to or subtracting from a stack of Victorian penny coins carried on the pendulum. The four clock faces – 23 feet (7 m) in diameter – were also designed by Pugin. The famous Westminster chimes are based on a phrase from Handel's 'I know that my redeemer liveth' and were copied from Great St Mary's Church in Cambridge. In the lantern at the top of the Elizabeth Tower is the Ayrton Light, which is lit after dark to indicate that either the Lords or the Commons are sitting. Named after a later Commissioner for Works, Acton Ayrton, it was installed in 1885 on the orders of Queen Victoria so that she could see from Buckingham Palace that her Parliament was at work.

The interior rooms of the Houses of Parliament were designed mainly by Pugin around themes from English history and contain statues, sculptures, murals, frescoes, stained-glass windows and other decorations by Victorian artists, such as John Birnie Philip, Charles West Cope, G.F. Watts and John Tenniel. Rarely seen is the Chapel of St Mary Undercroft beneath Westminster Hall, which was decorated in gorgeous polychrome High Victorian style by Sir Charles Barry's son Edward between 1860 and 1870.

Now walk back over Westminster Bridge for Westminster Station, noting as you go Norman Shaw's most famous work, the banded red-brick and Portland stone New Scotland Yard on the Victoria Embankment, built as headquarters for the Metropolitan Police in 1887.

Just around the corner from the station, in Parliament Street, is the Red Lion pub, refurbished in 1890 and another haunt of Charles Dickens and Victorian politicians.

End of walks: Westminster Station

Recommended Places for Refreshment

Audley Hotel 41–43 Mount St, W1

The Red Lion 2 Duke of York Street, SW1

The Golden Lion 25 King Street, SW1

The Albert 52 Victoria Street, SW1

The Cask and Glass 39–41 Palace Street, W1

The Windsor Castle 23 Francis Street, SW1

The Clarence 53 Whitehall, SW1

The Old Shades 37 Whitehall, SW1

The Silver Cross Tavern 33 Whitehall, SW1

The Sherlock Holmes 10 Northumberland Street, WC2

The Red Lion 48 Parliament Street, SW1

Victorian Architects, Engineers & Philanthropists

Aitchison, George (1825–1910)
Leighton House, Holland Park Road
59–61 Mark Lane, Whitechapel

Barry, Edward Middleton (1830–1880), 2nd son of Sir Charles Barry
Royal Opera House
Charing Cross Hotel and Eleanor Cross
Cannon Street Hotel (demolished)
St Christopher's Chapel, Great Ormond Street Hospital
Temple Gardens
St Giles National Schools, Endell Street
Burlington House, Piccadilly (with Robert Banks)

Barry, Sir Charles (1795–1860)
Houses of Parliament and Parliament Square
Travellers Club, Pall Mall
Reform Club, Pall Mall
Trafalgar Square
Bridgewater House, Cleveland Row

Barry Jr. Charles (1823–1900), eldest son of Sir Charles Barry
Great Eastern Hotel, Liverpool Street.

Basevi, George (1794–1845), architect of *Smith's Charity Estate, Brompton*

Egerton Crescent

Bentley, J.F. (1839–1902)
Westminster Cathedral
Presbytery of St Peter and St Edward Catholic Church, Palace
    Street

Blomfield, Sir Arthur (1829–1899)
Royal College of Music, South Kensington
Bank of England Law Courts Branch (The Old Bank of England
    pub), Fleet Street
87 Chancery Lane
Barclays Bank, Fleet Street
Oxford House, Derbyshire Street, Bethnal Green
Mission School (former), Floral Street, Covert Garden

Burges, William (1827–1881)
Tower House, Melbury Road

Butterfield, William (1814–1900)
All Saints, Margaret Street
St Augustine, Queen's Gate, South Kensington
St Alban the Martyr, Holborn
St Michael's Vicarage, Covent Garden

Clarke, Thomas Chatfield (1829–1895)
66–67 Cornhill
25 Throgmorton Street

Cole, Lieutenant H.H. (1843–1916), eldest son of Henry Cole

Royal College of Organists

Collcutt, Thomas (1840–1924)
The Queen's Tower (Imperial Institute)
Savoy Hotel
Palace Theatre
Lloyds Register of Shipping

Darbishire, Henry (1825–1899)
Peabody Buildings, Commercial Street
Peabody Buildings, Kemble Street
Manning House, Carlisle Street, Victoria
St Francis Friary, Francis Street, Victoria
Rochester Buildings, Old Pye Street, Victoria
Abbey Orchard Street Estate, Old Pye Street
Columbia Market (now demolished), Bethnal Green

Doll, Charles Fitzroy (1850–1929)
Russell Hotel

Fowke, Captain Francis (1823–1865)
Sheepshanks Gallery V&A
Royal Albert Hall

George, Sir Ernest (1839–1922)
50 Cadogan Square, South Kensington
1–18a Collingham Gardens, Kensington (with Harold Peto)
20–26 Harrington Gardens, Kensington (with Harold Peto)
35–45 Harrington Gardens, Kensington (with Harold Peto)
1–5 Mount Street, Mayfair (with Harold Peto)

104 –113 Mount Street, Mayfair (with Harold Peto)
Thomas Goode & Co.Ltd, South Audley Street, Mayfair

Gibson, John (1817–1892)
National Provincial Bank, Bishopsgate (Gibson Hall)
Child & Co, Fleet Street
Bloomsbury Central Baptist Chapel
Nigeria House, Northumberland Avenue

Hardwick, Philip (1792–1870)
Great Hall and Library Lincoln's Inn

Hardwick, P.C. (1822–1892), son of Philip Hardwick
Gateway for Lincoln's Inn
2 Palace Gate, Kensington (for John Millais)

Jones, Sir Horace (1819–1887)
Smithfield Market
Temple Bar Memorial, Fleet Street
Leadenhall Market
Tower Bridge

Knowles, James (1804–1884)
Grosvenor Hotel, Victoria Station (with his son)

Knowles, James Jr (1831–1908)
Mark Masons' Hall, 86 St James's Street
Grosvenor Hotel, Victoria Station (with his father)

Mackmurdo, Arthur Heygate (1851–1942)
25 Cadogan Gardens, South Kensington

Pearson, John Loughborough (1817–1897)
Two Temple Place (Astor House)

Pennethorne, Sir James (1801–1871)
New Oxford Street
Public Record Office, Chancery Lane
No. 10 Buckingham Gate, westminster
Buckingham Palace Ballroom

Phipps, C.J. (1835–1897)
Vaudeville Theatre
Savoy Theatre
Garrick Theatre
Devonshire Club (restyled), St James's Street

Pugin, Augustus (1812–1852)
Houses of Parliament (Interior)
Elizabeth Tower (Great Clock Tower)
Clock faces Big Ben (Great Clock)
Church of the Immaculate Conception, Farm Street (high altar
  and reredos)

Ricardo, Halsey (1854–1928)
55 and 57 Melbury Road
Perrin Gallery, Leighton House

Roberts, Henry (1803–1876) *Honorary Architect for*
Society for Improving the Condition of the Labouring Classes and
Metropolitan Association for Improving the Dwellings of the Industrious
Classes
Parnell House (for SICLC)
Victoria Cottages, Deal Street, Whitechapel

Roumieu, Robert Lewis (1814–1877)
33–35 Eastcheap

Scott, Sir George Gilbert (1811–1878)
Albert Memorial
St Mary Abbots, Kensington
St Michael, Cornhill (porch)
Foreign and Commonwealth Office
Grand Midland Hotel, St Pancras
Library Lincoln's Inn (extension)

Sedding, John Dando (1838–1891)
Holy Trinity, Sloane Square

Shaw, Norman (1831–1912)
Lowther Lodge, Kensington
Albert Hall Mansions
62, 68, 72 Cadogan Square
8 and 31 (Woodland House) Melbury Road
170 and 196 Queen's Gate, South Kensington
Corner of St James's Street and Pall Mall
Norman Shaw Buildings (New Scotland Yard)

Smirke, Sydney (1798–1877)
Burlington House (Exhibition Galleries)
Conservative Club, 78 St James's Street (now a bank)
Oxford and Cambridge Club, Pall Mall (with brother Sir Robert
    Smirke)

Smith, Sidney (1858–1913)
Cripplegate Institute, Golden Lane, City

Stevenson, J.J. (1831–1908)
Jamaica High Commission, Exhibition Road
40–42 Pont Street, South Kensington
South Side Cadogan Square, South Kensington
8 Palace Gate, Kensington
East side and island sites Kensington Court

Street, G.E. (1824–1881)
4 Cadogan Square, South Kensington
Royal Courts of Justice

Taylor, Sir John (1833–1912)
Public Record Office, Chancery Lane
Bow Street Magistrate's Court

Tite, Sir William (1798–1873)
Royal Exchange

Townsend, Charles Harrison (1851–1928)
Bishopsgate Institute
Whitechapel Art Gallery

Verity, Frank (1864–1937) (Son of Thomas Verity)
Beefsteak Club, Irving Street, Whitehall
St John's Hospital (former), Lisle Street, Soho

Verity, Thomas (1837–1891)
Criterion Theatre and Restaurant
Audley Hotel, Mayfair

Vulliamy, George (1817–1886)
Victoria Embankment lamp-posts
Sphinxes, Cleopatra's Needle, Victoria Embankment
Swiss Protestant Church, Endell Street
Charing Cross Road and Shaftesbury Avenue
164 Bishopsgate, Spitalfields

Waterhouse, Sir Alfred (1830–1905)
Natural History Museum
Mappin & Webb, 1a Old Bond Street
National Liberal Club, Whitehall Place
Prudential Assurance Building, Holborn
King's Weigh House Church, Duke Street, Mayfair
University College Hospital

Webb, Aston (1849–1930)
French Protestant Church, Soho Square
Victoria & Albert Museum Main Building
13–15 Moorgate

Webb, Philip (1831–1915)
14 Holland Park Road

91–101 Worship Street, Shoreditch
1 Palace Green, Kensington

Engineers

Bazalgette, Sir Joseph (1819–1891)
Victoria Embankment
Charing Cross Road and Shaftesbury Avenue
Northumberland Avenue

Cubitt, James (1836–1912)
Welsh Presbyterian Church

Cubitt, Joseph (1811–1872), nephew of Lewis Cubitt
First Blackfriars Railway Bridge and road bridge

Cubitt, Lewis (1799–1883) (brother of Thomas Cubitt)
Kings Cross Station and Great Northern Hotel

Hawkshaw, Sir John (1811–1891)
Charing Cross Station
Hungerford Bridge
Cannon Street Station (original)

Wolfe-Barry, Sir John (1836–1918), 4th son of Sir Charles Barry
Cannon Street Railway Bridge (with Sir John Hawkshaw)
Second Blackfriars Railway Bridge
Tower Bridge

Philanthropists

Peabody, George (1795–1869) *Banker (business later became J.P.Morgan)*
Founder: Peabody Trust

Waterlow, Sir Sydney (1822–1908) *Printer and Banker,*
Chairman: Improved Industrial Dwellings Company
Cobden Buildings, Kings Cross Road
Wilmot Street, Bethnal Green
Leopold Buildings, Columbia Road
Coburg Buildings, Francis Street, Victoria

Index of People

INDEX OF PEOPLE

INDEX OF PEOPLE

INDEX OF PEOPLE

Index of Places

References

Hobhouse, H. (ed.), 'Colby Court, Kensington House and Kensington Court', *Survey of London Kensington Square to Earl's Court*, 42 (1986), 55-76.

Sheppard, F. H. W. (ed.), 'Hyde Park and Kensington Gate', *Survey of London South Kensington Museums Area*, 38 (1975), 26-38.

Sheppard, F. H.W. (ed.), 'Palace Gate', *Survey of London South Kensington Museums Area*, 42 (1975), 38-48.

These journals can all be accessed through British History Online.